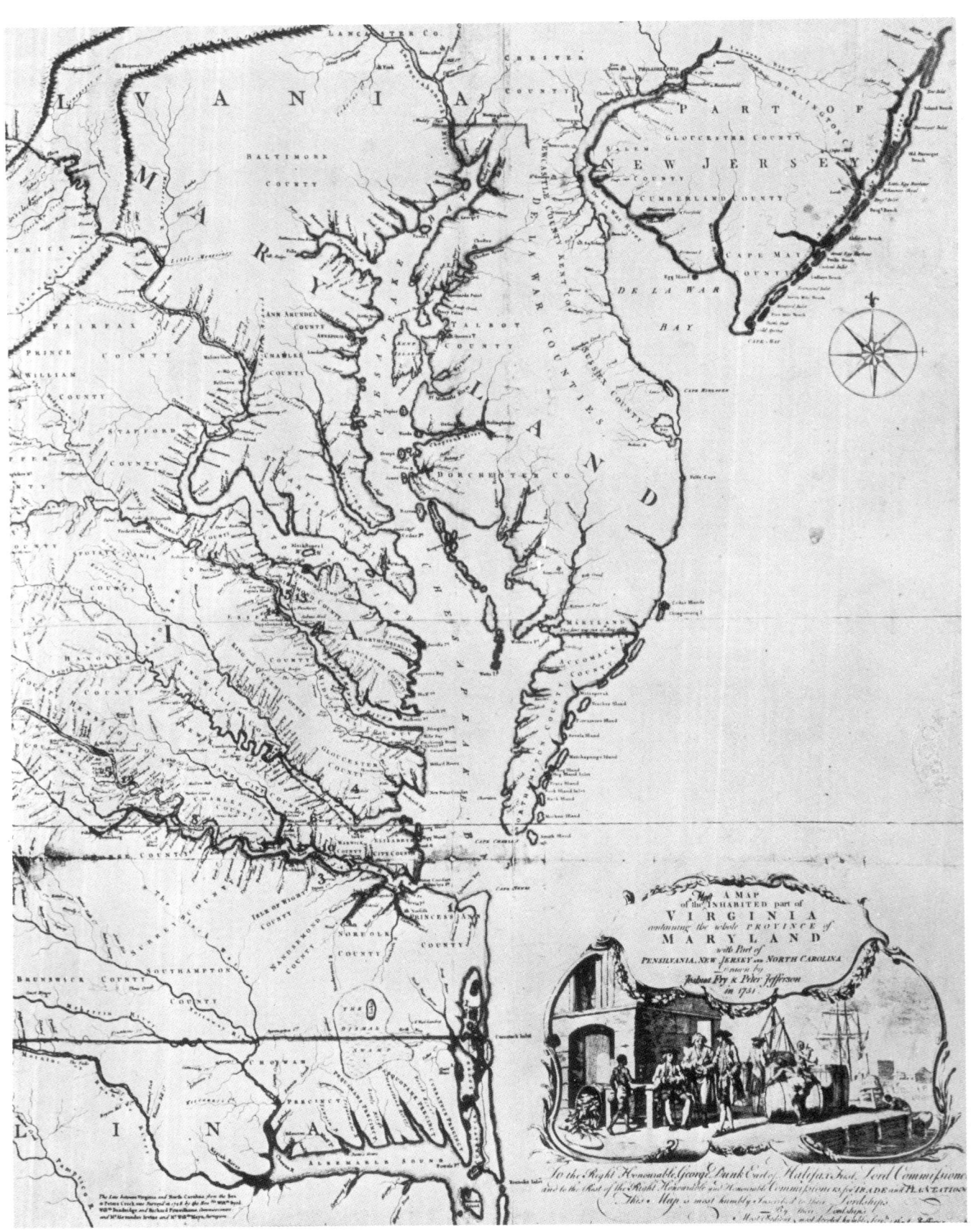

HALF OF A MAP MADE IN 1751 BY JOSHUA FRY AND PETER JEFFERSON

The numbers indicate the locations of the fifteen houses described in this volume: 1—Thoroughgood House; 2—Greenspring; 3—Bacon's Castle; 4—Fairfield; 5—Ampthill; 6—President's House; 7—Stratford; 8—Westover; 9—Rosewell; 10—Carter's Grove; 11—Cleve; 12—Wilton; 13—Mount Airy; 14—Blandfield; 15—Menokin

DOMESTIC COLONIAL ARCHITECTURE OF TIDEWATER VIRGINIA

By
THOMAS TILESTON WATERMAN
and
JOHN A. BARROWS

With an Introduction by
FISKE KIMBALL

DOVER PUBLICATIONS, INC.
NEW YORK

A Note on the Scale Drawings in this Edition

The drawings of details that were reproduced full-size in the original edition (pages 163-175) have been reduced by 15 per cent.

All other drawings have been reduced by .10 per cent, so that their scales are now as follows:

Drawings marked 3/32" to the foot are now 2.7/32" to the foot; i.e., one inch equals approximately 11' 10".

Drawings marked 1/4" to the foot are now .9/4" to the foot; i.e., one inch equals approximately 4' 5".

Drawings marked 3/64" to the foot are now 2.7/64" to the foot; i.e., one inch equals approximately 23' 8".

This Dover edition, first published in 1969, is an unabridged republication of the work originally published in 1932 by Charles Scribner's Sons.

The publisher is grateful to the Director of the Brooklyn Public Library for making a copy of this work available for the purpose of reproduction.

Standard Book Number: 486-22356-6
Library of Congress Catalog Card Number: 79-91975

Manufactured in the United States of America
Dover Publications, Inc.
180 Varick Street
New York, N.Y. 10014

TO
OUR MOTHERS
ANNE CAMPBELL WATERMAN
AND
MIRIAM COBB BARROWS

Contents

The Adam Thoroughgood House, 1636–1640, Princess Anne County
Page 1

Greenspring, 1642–1676, James City County
Page 9

Bacon's Castle, 1650–1676, Surry County
Page 19

Fairfield, 1692, Gloucester County
Page 29

Ampthill, Before 1732, Chesterfield County
Page 37

The President's House, 1732, Williamsburg
Page 49

Stratford, 1725–1730, Westmoreland County
Page 57

Westover, 1726, Charles City County
Page 69

Rosewell, 1720–1730, Gloucester County
Page 85

Carter's Grove, 1751, James City County
Page 97

Cleve, 1754, King George County
Page 109

Wilton, 1754, Henrico County
Page 117

Contents

Mount Airy, 1758, Richmond County
Page 125

Blandfield, 1760–1770, Essex County
Page 139

Menokin, 1769, Richmond County
Page 149

Details of Profiles
Page 161

Table of Brick Sizes
Page 177

A Comparison of Outline Plans
Page 179

Glossary of Architectural Terms
Page 185

Index
Page 189

Introduction

THAT the great plantation houses of the Virginia Tidewater should have hitherto lacked exact study is surprising, but it is true. By those who know the Tidewater it will be readily understood. Standing by the riversides in vast stretches of coastal territory where communication was once almost solely by water, approached from the land mainly on horseback over roads which until recently were frequently almost impassable to vehicles, they lay in a country devastated by early exhaustion of the soil, by the ravages of invasion and war, and by the destruction of slavery on which rested their whole economy. Almost without towns, which formed no important part of the old self-contained plantation system, almost without inns, which plantation hospitality rendered unnecessary in the travels of a gentleman, they have remained deeply inaccessible to the hurried architect of an industrial world.

A few houses, to be sure, fortunately placed near the growing urban centres, early attracted visiting students. Westover and Shirley owed their exclusive early fame little more to their own magnificence than to their being within reach from Richmond for a hasty trip with camera and rule. Blandfield and Stratford were as imposing in their distant retreats; Rosewell, Mount Airy, and Cleve were once as richly finished, before fire gutted them in their succorless isolation.

When the river steamboats, their last contact with the modern world, were stilled by the automobile, oblivion seemed closing over these houses and their ruins. But the automobile has made its own amends, bringing roads and a new accessibility by land, a new opportunity for patient and prolonged study. Its maturer fruits are first largely offered in this book.

The pioneer student of a generation ago made hasty measurements, guessed heights, finished his drawings far from the possibility of verification, forgot out-buildings, neglected to note materials and colors. To this day architects using the older works generally suppose the doorways of Westover to be of wood. Pretty are the theories which have been built on such premises! The vast plane surfaces of houses like Carter's Grove have seemed barren to those who were not informed of the rich variety of color and gauging in their brickwork, and which, unlike mouldings, did not appear in summary outline drawings. Hasty examination did not reveal those evidences of progressive enlargement which, at Ampthill and elsewhere, explain so much.

The authors of this book have given long and loving study of such subtle qualities and evidences. Charred ruins and bare surfaces here come to life and glow under their touch. A whole province of great mansions, most of them never drawn or published before, is rediscovered. The background of a vanished civilization is exactly set forth.

FISKE KIMBALL

Foreword

TIDEWATER Virginia formed a background against which took place a great pageant of events in Colonial History from the arrival of the colonists in 1607 at Jamestown to the surrender at Yorktown in 1781. The very isolation that its great tidal rivers created has preserved until our time a section of the country intimately interwoven with the lives of the great men and women of the Colonial Period, amazingly unchanged and retaining in its countryside the flavor of times long gone. Though war and fire have left their impress on it, and many houses are now only names, others with their dependencies, plantation buildings, tree-bordered avenues and boxwood gardens remain to give us an insight into the personalities of the makers of our early history. The byways, brilliant with surfaces of red clay and bordered by stately rows of cedars and hollies, have a feeling of remoteness that brings the past very near. Not only their houses and estates remain to give color to the lives of early Virginians, but also their court city of Williamsburg, spared the destruction that progress would have brought it; their parish churches surrounded by majestic rows of tombs, rich with heraldry; their courthouses heavy with imposing names that loyalty to the Royal house inspired. The stage is set for a play that will never be enacted again.

A Renaissance with its attendant modernisms of fine highways and bridges for the ubiquitous automobile has brought new life to the Tidewater. Great houses, long fallen from their high estate, have come to new owners and new prosperity; the Capitol of the Colony, the Palace of the Royal Governor, and the Main Building of the College of William and Mary are rising from their ashes and excavations are bringing to life important buildings almost forgotten.

These eastern counties form a field fertile in interest for antiquarians and architects. Their buildings comprise a page of greatest importance in the history of the architecture of the American Colonies, but, when this history is finally written, it must be based on a realization that, in common with the architecture of European countries, it has countless local phases and mannerisms. Until regional architecture of the United States is examined and catalogued, a comprehensive survey of our early building will be impossible. New England and Pennsylvania have been well covered with both measured drawings and photographs. New York, New Jersey, and the Southern States have only been touched upon. This is particularly true of Virginia, where practically all of the notable buildings have been difficult of access and widely separated. Such houses are Westover,

Foreword

Carter's Grove, and Stratford—all familiar from photographs and descriptions which sometimes unfortunately have been of such a nature as to make it difficult to arrive at a conclusion regarding their genesis and evolution. Students who were unable to visit the buildings themselves frequently found it impossible to correlate the information they already had at their disposal.

It has been the aim of the authors to present, as comprehensively as space will allow, measured drawings and photographs of a related group of domestic buildings of Tidewater Virginia, arranged chronologically, that they may be susceptible of classification and study. To present even so limited a number as those contained herein, it has been necessary to omit plans and details of interior finish in favor of small-scale elevations of the main buildings, and their immediate subsidiaries, where such exist. These small-scale drawings show the buildings restored to their probable original condition. In order to differentiate the existing fabrics and the restored features, larger-scale details have also been presented of the houses as they actually exist. This latter practice has been departed from only in the case of Cleve, which was burned and demolished above the water-table in 1917. This detail drawing, on which the restoration was based, was determined by old photographs, measurements of the basement, and of the derelict stone from the house which is piled nearby. In the detail of Rosewell, the portion of the pediment over the doorway that fell has been shown restored; as has the pier to the left of the central window on the third floor. In all other cases, except for the omission of modern porches concealing original features, all buildings are shown as they exist. Full-size profiles of important mouldings are also included. The small number of great plan compositions makes it unsafe to generalize as to the development of the formal plan. It has seemed wise, however, to append plans in profile at small scale for comparison.

The fifteen houses illustrated here are situated in that part of the State contiguous to Chesapeake Bay and the four great semitidal rivers: James, York, Rappahannock, and Potomac. The rivers in the early days were often the only means of communication, and the houses were built near them, for the roads that existed were frequently impassable. On the James and York they were usually situated on the banks of the river; but on the Rappahannock they were usually placed on the lateral ridges that parallel it a mile or more distant.

Social conditions in Virginia dictated an architecture entirely different from that of the rest of the country, except South Carolina and Maryland. The great plantation houses, with their dependencies, were self-contained units, completely isolated, except for the neighboring mansions, perhaps several miles away. The farmhouse, familiar to the North, almost did not exist in Tidewater Virginia after 1700; its only architectural equivalent being the town houses of the landed aristocracy in Williamsburg. These, in some cases, were not as large as the minor buildings on the important estates.

Great wealth, traditions of living brought from England, and close contact with the

Foreword

mother country, brought the Georgian period to an early flowering in the Tidewater. Extravagantly lofty apartments, such as those over fourteen feet high in the Governor's Palace (1705), Williamsburg, probably here superseded the low-ceilinged room of the Jacobean Period sooner than elsewhere in the colonies. That in these latter sliding sash was used originally is not known, but in 1699 it was directed that the sash windows be used in the Capitol to be built in Williamsburg, and this innovation was undoubtedly followed immediately in the more important domestic work. The gables of the earlier times were replaced by hip roofs with horizontal cornices at the College of William and Mary (1695), Fairfield (1692), and at the Capitol (1701). No transitional features remain in Ampthill, Rosewell, Westover, or Stratford—the earliest of the existing Georgian houses. The President's House, in this volume placed earlier in order than the three latter—though later in date—is a counterpart of Brafferton Hall, in which a brick remains dated 1723. Ampthill, traditionally dated 1732, is shown first among the Georgian houses for reasons discussed in the text accompanying it.

The material of which the first colonists of Virginia built their houses probably was largely wood, although brick is known to have been used very early. No wood house of the seventeenth century is known to survive in the State—with the possible exception of the Galt House in Williamsburg. At least two brick houses remain complete, however, the Thoroughgood House and Bacon's Castle. In these, except the front of the former, the brick is laid in English bond, with no stone or rubbed-brick dressings. English bond seems to have been the characteristic seventeenth-century bond, though St. Luke's Church, Isle of Wight County, is undeniably very early, perhaps 1632, as claimed; and it, together with Fairfield (1692), Gloucester County, is laid in Flemish bond. Below the water-table at Fairfield the bond used is English, and this combination of bonds, Flemish above the water-table and English below, is the typical arrangement almost throughout the eighteenth century; it appearing in a dated example as late as 1769 in the Court House at Williamsburg. An infrequent variant is the use of Flemish bond both above and below the water-table. Whether the complete English bond wall surface at Ampthill is a sporadic reoccurrence of an old method, or whether the house is really one of that group of buildings of English bond which, with almost no exception, falls within the seventeenth century, has not been established. If it is of the latter period, it would be the first house in Virginia to have rubbed dressings; i. e., jambs, corners, and architectural features of brick varying in color from the wall toward vermilion and rubbed against a rubbing-stone to produce a very smooth surface. At Ampthill the dressings are of the simplest type, being only one stretcher, alternating vertically with a header, in width. The President's House and Westover also have this minimum rubbed work, but Rosewell—if it be earlier than Stratford—established the precedent of very rich rubbed dressings; in fact, the maximum richness (a stretcher, header and closer deep) which

Foreword

lasted in the great houses throughout the period.

Stone was much used for architectural features: steps, gate posts, window trim, etc. This material is, undoubtedly, identical with English Portland stone, which is known to have been frequently imported from Bristol, England, the port of lading. In the Journal of the House of Burgesses it is directed that stone for the Capitol be brought from England.

A gold-brown stone was used on the Rappahannock at Mount Airy and Menokin, and this is said to have been quarried on the estates. At Mount Airy some Aquia Creek stone, from near Stafford County Court House, was used, as well as imported stone. The two houses mentioned above are entirely of stone, as is Prestwould, Mecklenburg County; but aside from these, brick and wood are used universally throughout the Tidewater.

English influence on architecture came directly in the form of imported labor; e. g., the committee for building the Capitol sent to England in August, 1700, for three bricklayers and three carpenters. Clerks of the works were sometimes brought from England to oversee the erection of elaborate buildings. Thomas Hadley came in 1695 to direct the work on the College of William and Mary, and David Minitree to supervise the building of Carter's Grove in 1751. These men, as well as others of whom record does not remain, were probably architects as well as overseers and had influence on, if not complete charge of, the designs themselves. Some houses, especially Rosewell, show undeniable architectonic character which would not result from the efforts of an amateur. Various traditions of Wren designs in Virginia have been found to lack confirmation, however, and so must be largely discounted.

The estates of the Tidewater are connected by an inextricable web of intermarriages and relationships, which give them all a bearing on one another. These family connections are not the least of the interest of the great houses, and they have been referred to briefly in the chapters accompanying the various houses, together with relevant historic facts.

With the reawakening of interest throughout the country in the Colonial architecture of Virginia, it is hoped that the materials gathered here may be helpful, both to the architect and the layman. Especially to the former, many details in the treatment of brickwork and stonework will be of interest; together with the scale, general composition, and grouping of the main buildings and their dependencies, and the profiles of the important mouldings.

The authors take this opportunity of thanking the owners of the houses illustrated for their unfailing kindness, courtesy, and assistance in obtaining the data used in the preparation of this book. Thanks are due particularly to Miss Keeler of Lynnhaven Farm, Mr. Dimmock of Greenspring, the du Pont Rayon Co. of Ampthill, Doctor J. A. C. Chandler, of the College of William and Mary, Mr. Richard Crane of Westover, Mr. Charles E. Stuart of Stratford, Captain Greaves of Rosewell, Mr. and Mrs.

Foreword

Hunsdon Cary of Ampthill, Mr. Lewis of Cleve, the Misses Tayloe of Mount Airy, the Messrs. Beverley of Blandfield, and Mr. and Mrs. Bellfield of Menokin. The authors also wish to express their gratitude for invaluable assistance rendered by the following: Professor Fiske Kimball; Mr. Robert Bellows; Mr. Lawrence Kocher; Mr. William G. Perry, Mr. Thomas Mott Shaw, and Mr. Andrew Hepburn of Perry, Shaw & Hepburn; Lyon G. Tyler, LL.D., President Emeritus of the College of William and Mary; the Rev. W. A. R. Goodwin, D.D.; E. G. Swem, Librarian of the College of William and Mary; Mrs. Harrison Wellford of Sabine Hall; Mrs. Lamb of Belleville; the Rev. Donald MacDonald-Millar; Mr. Walter Macomber; Mr. F. C. Baldwin; Miss Mary Goodwin; Miss Estelle Smith; Miss Elizabeth Hayes; Miss Lucy Burrows; the Virginia State Chamber of Commerce; Mr. Thomas T. Layton; the Rev. W. H. T. Squires; Messrs. David Hayes, Joseph Kenney and Stockton Rouzie.

Thomas T. Waterman
John A. Barrows.

The Adam Thoroughgood House

Courtesy of the Virginia State Chamber of Commerce

THE ADAM THOROUGHGOOD HOUSE, WEST FRONT

The Adam Thoroughgood House
LYNNHAVEN RIVER, PRINCESS ANNE COUNTY
1636-1640

IT is appropriate that the oldest existing house in Virginia, and in all probability the oldest house in English-speaking America, should be small and unpretentious. It is appropriate, too, that it should be of brick, a progenitor of the great masonry houses of the eighteenth century. In 1636 Adam Thoroughgood came to the shores of quiet Lynnhaven Bay, having patented a parcel of land which in 1637 was described as embracing 5,350 acres.

Adam Thoroughgood was from Lynn, England, from which Lynnhaven Bay derived its name. He was the brother of Sir John Thoroughgood, but came to Virginia in the ship *Charles* as an indentured servant in 1621. He apparently worked off his passage money quickly, for he became a man of position and sat as a burgess in the Assembly as early as 1629.

Princess Anne County at that date was part of Elizabeth City County. Life here was perilous, being subject from the land to Indian raids and from the sea to the raids of pirates that infested the waters about the Capes until well into the eighteenth century. But Adam and his good wife Sarah Offley attended to the numerous duties of pioneering and found time to build a comfortable home for themselves and their family. At his death in 1640 Thoroughgood left this house to his widow.

His will describes it as being a brick dwelling, and though the existing building cannot be definitely established as the same, the evidence is extremely strong—even to the letters "A*d*. T." cut quaintly on a brick in the walls of the dwelling. A brick also remains with an illegible date upon it, which is said to have read 1640 some twenty years ago, before the surface disintegrated. Here Adam Thoroughgood's descendants lived until the middle of the nineteenth century, when the home was sold and fell on evil days. It was finally rescued from a precarious existence as a negro's farmhouse by the present owner, by whom it has been carefully repaired.

The lawns that surround it, the box, and the ivy, are much too nearly perfect to recall the lean pioneer days, but they harmonize well with the sashes of the eighteenth century which have supplanted the earlier casements. The house boasts only four rooms, two to a floor, those above being under the steep roof, now pierced with dormers of distinct Georgian character, but originally probably lit only by the diminutive openings in the gables. The home of the Burgess is extremely modest and displays no more architectural elegance than the magnificent chimney at the south end. Its great base, the length of which is 11 feet, diminishes by bold

Domestic Colonial Architecture of Tidewater Virginia

weatherings to 3 feet at the top, and its projection from the wall diminishes by horizontal offsets at the bottom and top of the lateral weatherings. These are protected from disintegration by brick and tile laid flat upon them.

The broad face of the chimney is traversed by four belt courses; the three lowest are laid in Flemish bond with glazed headers, in contrast to the English bond of the rest of the stack. The intermediate course carries across the whole gable, defining the second-floor line, and this treatment is similarly repeated on the north gable, though here the chimney is built within the walls of the house and has no projection. Like the freestanding stack, it is T-shaped above the ridge, being the same height and approximately the same size. Glazed headers are used on both gables just below and paralleling the barge-board, to emphasize the rake of the roof. This seventeenth-century decoration persisted into the middle of the eighteenth century, where in the dependencies of Carter's Grove (1751), James City County, it is again repeated.

As at Sweet Hall, King William County, three walls of the Thoroughgood house are laid in English bond, but the front wall, apparently of the same date, is Flemish bond. There is no sign of a joint to indicate that the work is later, nor is the brick size or character different from that of the rest of the house. The theory that Flemish bond was not used in the colony before 1700 is here, in perhaps the oldest house, apparently refuted. English bond seems to have been typical during the seventeenth century, for it is found in the jail, spring house, and other buildings contemporary with Greenspring (c. 1642), James City County; at the church tower, Jamestown, 1639–47; at Bacon's Castle, Surry County, 1657, and at the Main Building of the College of William and Mary, Williamsburg, 1695. If the wall is assumed to be original it will help to sustain the early date of the very mediæval-looking St. Luke's Church (1632?), Isle of Wight County. This building is entirely in Flemish bond, and while the date may be considered only tentative, the early character of the crow-stepped gables and tracery windows would strongly tend to substantiate it.

While examining the north wall, a narrow blocked-up opening was discovered, which, in all probability, contained an early casement window. The outer jamb of the modern first-floor window of the north gable, as well as that of the south, is approximately the same distance from the corner of the house as the jamb of the blocked opening. Within the house, panelling of eighteenth-century character covers the area formerly occupied by the bricked-up window. The Flemish-bond wall may have been built at the date of the installation of the Georgian panels and at the time the eighteenth-century openings were inserted to replace the small casements. The similarity in the distance of these jambs from corners makes it reasonable to assume that originally small windows flanked the chimneys on both ends of the house.

In the east wall a vertical series of seven or eight glazed headers are still in place, flanking the present double-hung windows. In height they closely coincide with that of the

The Adam Thoroughgood House

Cook

BEFORE RESTORATION   FROM THE NORTHEAST   DETAIL OF THE CHIMNEY

opening found in the north wall. These headers, it would seem, were a decorative feature, simulating the later rubbed work, used here to accent the jambs of the former casements. That this type of window was used is substantiated by the size of the openings at Bacon's Castle and Fairfield, and by a fragment of leaded glass found at Greenspring.

In the accompanying restoration of the building, the dormers are omitted because of their absence in other work of early date, and because of their obviously late detail. Small segmental windows in the south gable are made to replace the more modern ones, and correspond to those in the north gable. The transomed type of casement of the first floor is purely an assumption, but the leading is based upon that of similar design found at Greenspring. The segmental arches with glazed headers are precedented by the basement windows of the Main Building of the College of William and Mary. The door is a double-sheathed design, similar to one found at Fairfield. The larger-scale detail, half of one gable end and half of the other, indicates the position of the blocked opening in one drawing, and half the outline of the projecting chimney in the other.

Many points concerning the Thoroughgood House are still to be explained; further research may some day clarify them. In the meantime, Thoroughgood's will, the presence of a dwelling almost entirely of English bond, the mediæval character of the design, the evidence of casements, the presence of the initials "A*d*. T.," and the defaced-date brick will stand as substantial evidence of the early date of the house.

Domestic Colonial Architecture of Tidewater Virginia

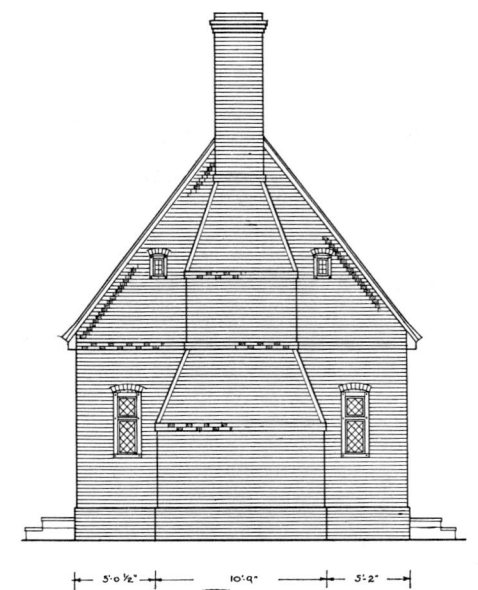

RESTORED SOUTH ELEVATION

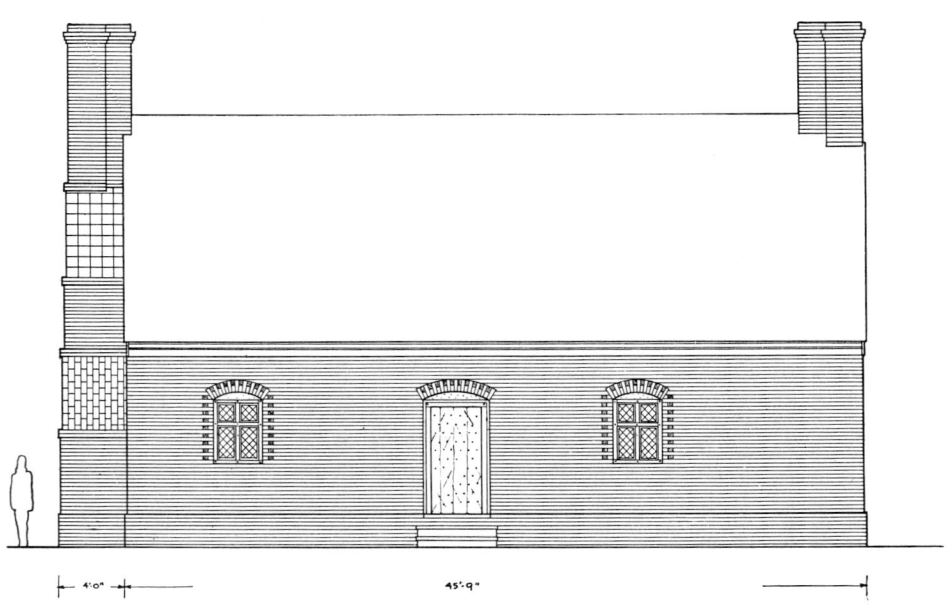

RESTORED EAST ELEVATION

Scale, $\frac{3}{32}$ in. to the foot

The Adam Thoroughgood House

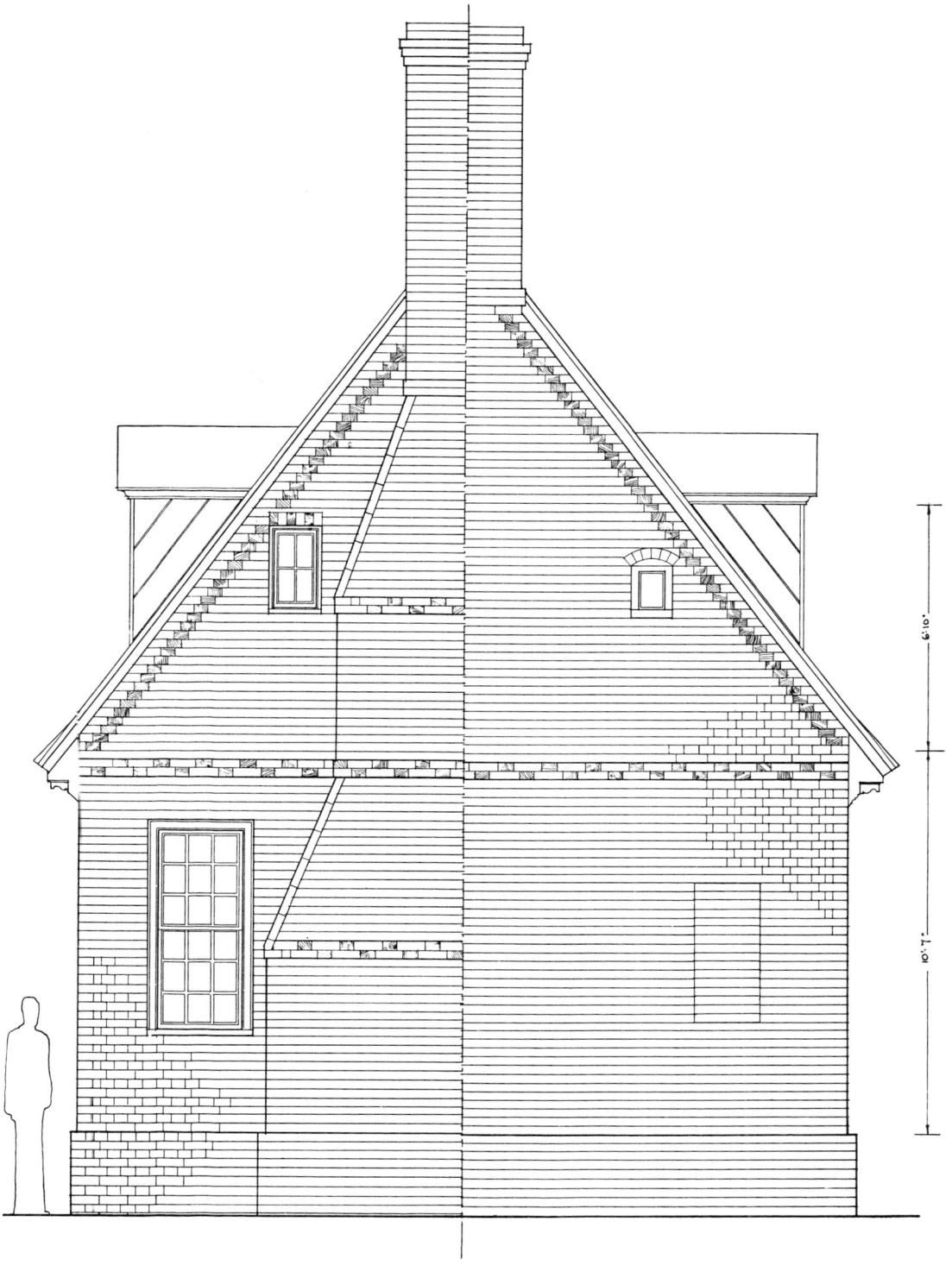

DETAIL OF ONE-HALF OF SOUTH (LEFT) AND NORTH ELEVATIONS
Scale, ¼ in. to the foot

Greenspring

FOUNDATION OF GREENSPRING, SIR WILLIAM BERKELEY'S HOUSE, JAMES CITY COUNTY

Greenspring

JAMES CITY COUNTY

1642-1676

THE first great house of the American Colonies was undoubtedly Greenspring, built by the Royal Governor of Virginia, Sir William Berkeley. The land upon which the house was erected, probably soon after 1642, was known as the Governor's Land and fronted on the James and Chickahominy Rivers, three miles above Jamestown. Here Berkeley lived until his recall in 1677, autocratically governing the colony with as little interference from the Burgesses as possible, and dispensing extravagant hospitality to the aristocracy of the colony and to refugee Royalists from England. Placing his own interests and those of his favorites before the welfare of the colony, and ignoring the depredations of the Indians, he finally brought upon himself the Rebellion of 1676, headed by Nathaniel Bacon. During this uprising the house was seized by Bacon and from its stores the forces besieging Jamestown were provisioned. It was the scene of an engagement during the Revolutionary War. The house stood until 1796, when it was taken down to make place for a new building designed by Benjamin Latrobe for William Ludwell Lee, to whom the property passed by descent from Colonel Phillip Ludwell I, second husband of Lady Berkeley. The Berkeley family later supplied another Royal Governor to Virginia, Norborne Berkeley, Lord Botetourt, much loved and remembered for his efforts in behalf of the colony in the days just before the Revolution.

Greenspring is not illustrative of the houses of the seventeenth century in Virginia, being unique as the product of conditions that applied to itself only. In the days preceding the lavish slave importations of the eighteenth century, land was cultivated on a system of comparatively small farms, by a class comparable to the yeomen of England. Shortly after 1700 slavery became a keystone in the economic life of the colony. Great houses then appeared in all the counties of Tidewater, and the era of building began.

Berkeley's house may still be traced in the foundations recently uncovered by the present owners. It has been stated that the smaller foundations to the east comprised the original structure, which was later superseded by the main building. This would seem improbable, inasmuch as the remaining walls bear no resemblance to any seventeenth-century plan. The main foundation, on the contrary, falls into a familiar category, although it is common to England rather than to this country. This would give a house 97 ft. 5 in. long by 24 ft. 9 in. wide. It contained three principal first-floor rooms in a single file, with an ell on the north front at the west end. Chimneys occurred in the east end and in the west partition wall as well as at the end of the ell.

It would be difficult to assign uses to the

Domestic Colonial Architecture of Tidewater Virginia

various rooms, but the kitchen may be assumed to have been within the house, not detached, as mediæval influence was still strong at the time of the building. It is possible that a quadrangle was contemplated, but never completed, as was actually the case with the Main Building of the College of William and Mary, in Williamsburg, built in 1695. This was so planned but stood as an L for forty years and was finally completed as a U. The foundations to the east at Greenspring may have been detached servants' quarters or gate houses, or may have terminated a later wing.

The brickwork of all walls shown on the accompanying plan is laid in English bond. Within the excavation was found a fragment of leaded glass in lozenge lights, the only known piece of original leaded glass in Virginia. This has been the precedent used in the restored glazing presented in the drawings of the Thoroughgood House, Bacon's Castle, and Fairfield. No sash is known to have been used in the colonies previous to 1700, although until the excavation of Greenspring no part of a casement had ever been found in Virginia; many, however, having come to light in New England.

Greenspring house stood at the crest of a high terrace above a plain, looking toward Jamestown. In the eighteenth century a great serpentine retaining wall was built against the rise, creating the north side of a forecourt with two terminal garden pavilions. The three remaining sides were enclosed and the foundations for these and further minor walls remain, laid in Flemish bond. The brickwork of the two pavilions survives in part, as does that of the seventeenth-century jail building. The forecourt treatment unearthed before the house is the most ambitious and monumental in Virginia.

Latrobe visited Greenspring in a professional capacity in 1796. At this time he made a sketch of the house, which is preserved in a private collection, at present inaccessible. It is described, however, as showing a two-story building with a high roof pierced by two tiers of dormers, as formerly at Bewdley, Lancaster County, c. 1700. The drawing of the alteration proposed by Latrobe is reproduced here. It is apparent that in his drawing he retained old openings on the principal floor, as they are not on axis with those above where he is unhampered. The basement he shows may be newly excavated or it may be the original first-floor wall, in which latter case the original building would have had two full stories.

Until the elevations have been determined Greenspring must remain conspicuous in American architecture as the longest plan of a domestic building known to have existed. In Virginia its nearest approach is Fairfield (1692), Gloucester County, which is 80 ft. 6 in. long, but extends over what was probably a group of buildings.

Extract from Pocket Diary of Benjamin H. Latrobe,
copied by fiske kimball, 1916

"IV. VIRGINIA, from Augt 3^d to Augt 26 1796." Richmond, Augt 3^d, 1796. (First two pages.)

On the 28th (July) I went in the stage to Williamsburg, where I found horses that car-

Greenspring

ried me to Mr. William Ludwell Lee's house at Greenspring about six miles SW of the city. . . . The principal part of Greenspring house was erected by Sir William Berkeley who was Governor of Virginia the latter end of the last century. (See Stith's and Beverley's History of Virginia.) It is a brick building of great solidity, but no attempt at grandeur. The lower story was covered by an arcade which is pulled down. The porch has some clumsy ornamental brick work about the style of James the first. . . .

It is Mr. Lee's intention to pull down the present mansion and to erect a modest Gentleman's house near this spot. The antiquity of the old house, if in any case, ought to plead in the project, but its inconvenience and deformity are more powerful advocates for its destruction. In it the oldest inhabited house in North America will disappear, for it was built in the Year 16—. Many of the first Virginian assemblies were held in the very room in which I was plotting the death of Muskitoes. . . .

GREENSPRING, FROM LATROBE'S DRAWING OF A PROPOSED ALTERATION

THE JAIL AT GREENSPRING

THE RUINS OF THE LEE HOUSE ON THE GREENSPRING ESTATE

Greensp

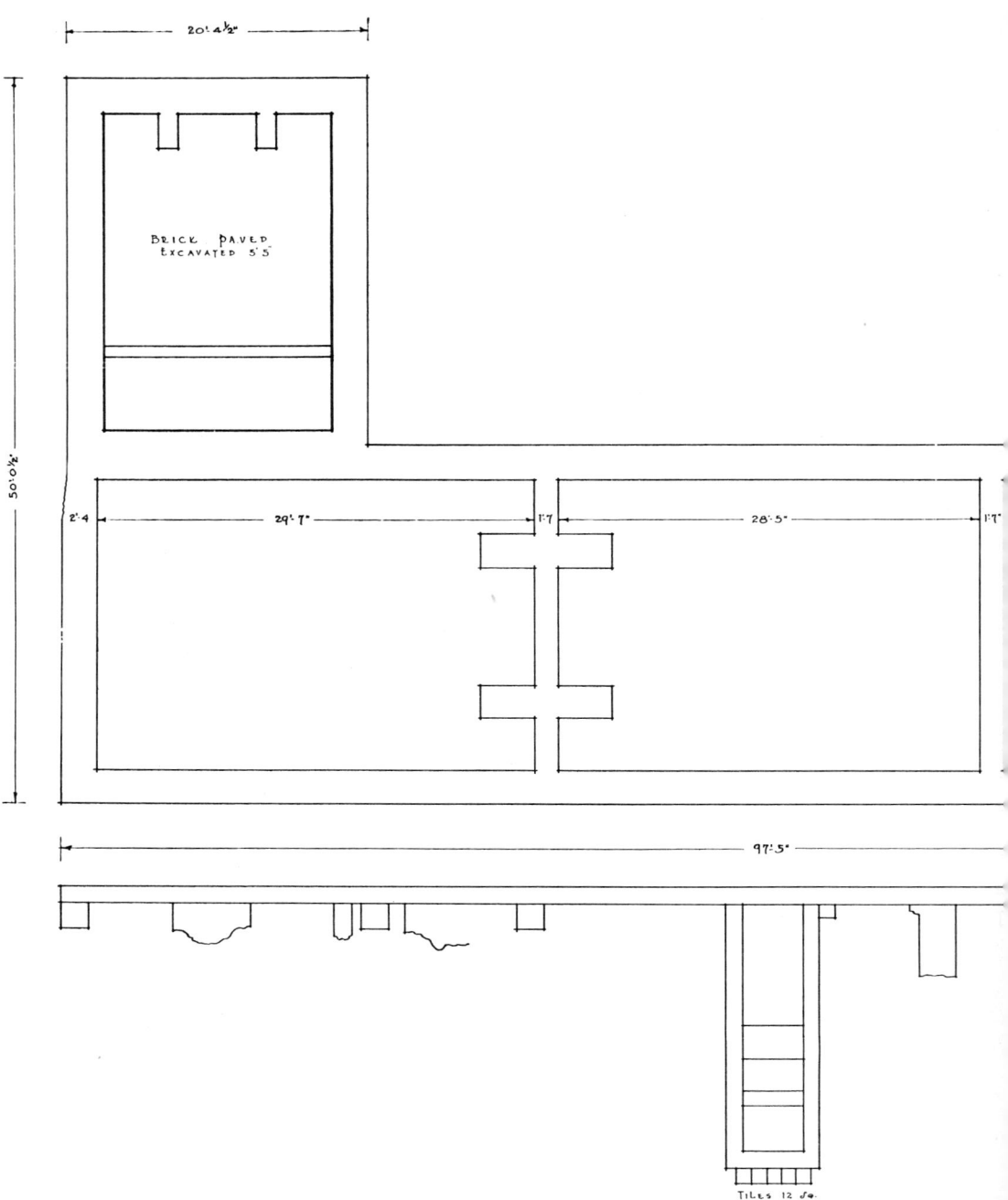

PLAN OF THE EXISTING FOUNDATIONS OF THE MAIN
Scale, $\tfrac{3}{32}$ in. to the foot

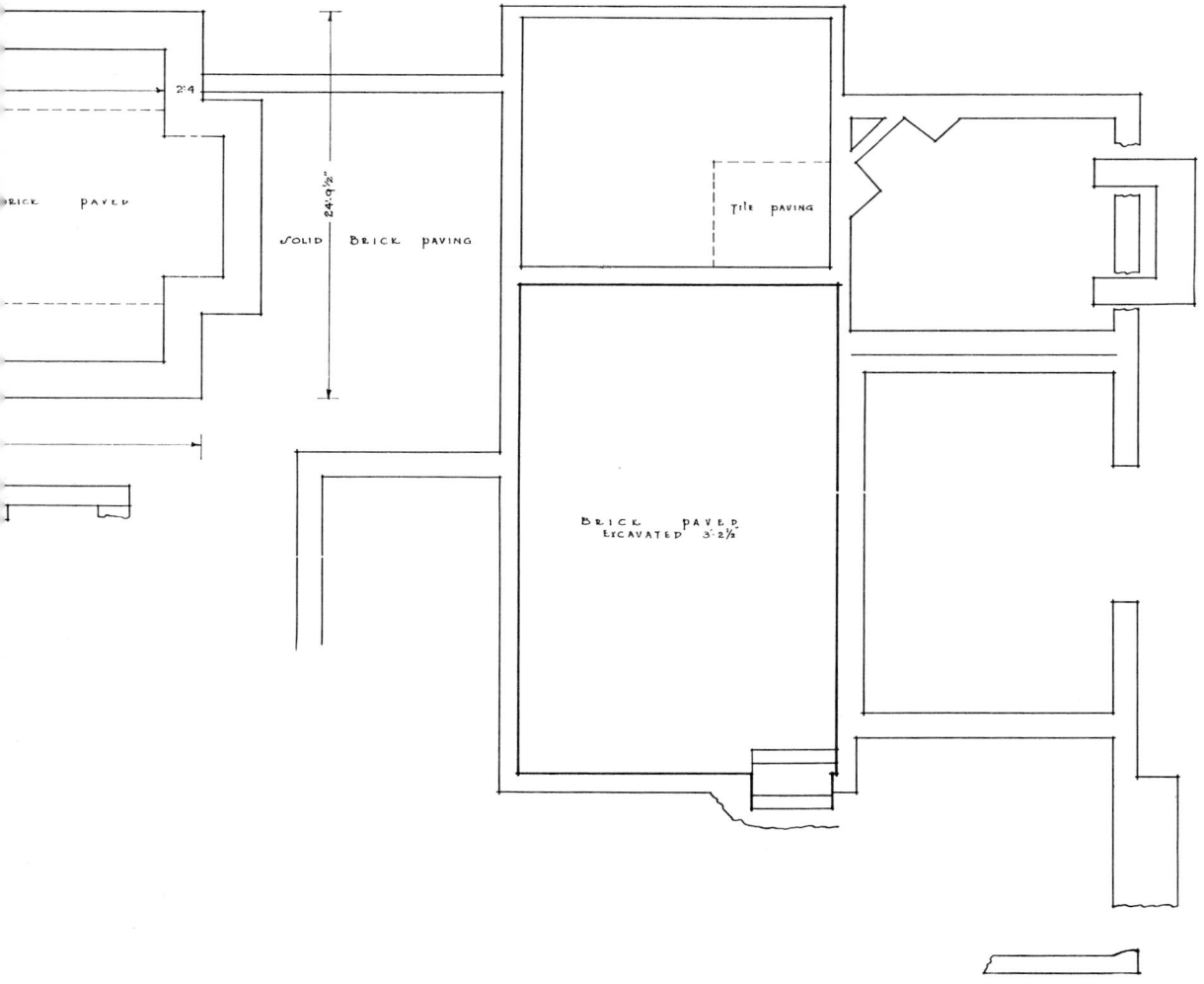

Bacon's Castle

BACON'S CASTLE, SURRY COUNTY

Bacon's Castle

SURRY COUNTY

Between 1650 and 1676

DISTINGUISHED by its association with a great event in Virginia's early history and by its unique architectural character, Bacon's Castle stands to-day much as it was built by the immigrant, Arthur Allen, probably soon after his arrival in Virginia in 1649. From the builder it passed to his son, a speaker of the House of Burgesses, from whom it was seized by adherents of Nathaniel Bacon, of Curles Neck, during the Rebellion of 1676. After the seizure it was garrisoned by sympathizers under William Rookings, and although Bacon is not even known to have visited the house, it has since been known as Bacon's Castle. It illustrates the advance in domestic architecture from the Thoroughgood House and was probably typical of the home of the better-class Virginia farmer of the last half of the seventeenth century. Except for a neo-Classic addition concealing one end and part of the front of the "Castle," the building has suffered little beyond the introduction of sash windows and the plastering of the face of the entrance tower.

The rectangular ground plan of the old house is only broken by the north and south towers, and by the boldly projecting end chimneys. The elevations are as simple as the plans, and the interest is largely confined to the high roofs of the towers, the splendid curvilinear gables, and the great triple chimney stacks. The ensemble of the house is a unique survival of seventeenth-century design.

The entire building, exclusive of the addition, is brick, laid in English bond, no glazed or rubbed brick being employed. Apparently the south front was once elaborately decorated with moulded and cut brickwork, but when the entrance door was changed from the south to the east of the tower, the projecting architectural features were cut back and the whole face plastered. At this time the brick trim around the second-floor windows was also plastered; its form, however, can still be determined. Narrow piers flank the openings, supporting lintels, or perhaps flat arches, enriched at the top with an ovolo moulding. The first-floor window jambs are unornamented, and the heads are formed by typical seventeenth-century segmental arches. Across the entire south front at the level of the second floor runs a projecting semicircular belt, two courses high. In contrast to this the water-table is simply an unmoulded three-inch offset.

Probably the west end of the building was originally devoid of openings or ornament below the third-floor line, the entire interest being confined to the gable and chimney treatment. Two windows have been cut in it

Domestic Colonial Architecture of Tidewater Virginia

recently and a tawdry addition containing a closet built to the north of the chimney. This latter has been omitted from the detail drawing as trivial. The great curvilinear gable springs from a corbelled parapet at the eaves, and sweeps up in a quadrant and a ramp to a semicircular termination surmounted by a small rectangular projection simulating a finial. All of the gables are covered by a coping of bricks laid flat across the parapet, and perhaps once protected by a plaster wash. The base of the south chimney diminishes in width by steep weatherings near the roof line, and three feet above this point both chimneys terminate in a wash, from which spring the triple stacks. The shafts are set diagonally to the base and stand independent of each other and of the gable behind, except where their caps engage. The caps are accented by bands of plaster between the upper offsets and a lower projection.

Admirable restored measured drawings of Bacon's Castle have already been made by Donald MacDonald-Millar. They closely coincide with the restoration included here, but on account of the value of the house as a transition between the Thoroughgood House and Fairfield it has seemed wise to present it again. The building has been remeasured with no appreciably different result than that obtained by Mr. Millar. The lower windows in the west face of the south tower and the east basement openings on the south front, however, were considered as probably not original. The transomed and mullioned casement windows are conjectural, based on coeval examples in the north, because of the lack of contemporary work in Virginia. The treatment of the ornamental brickwork on the entrance tower was obtained from an old woodcut. The embryonic pediment, found also at St. Luke's Church, Isle of Wight County, forms an interesting transitional feature as presaging the Georgian Period, while the degenerate label-mould recalls the past.

Bacon's Castle benefits from a site which intensifies the atmosphere of its great age. The gable end, with a long row of plantation dependencies stretching out beyond it, is seen at a distance across flat meadows. Approach is by a country lane, bordered by cedars and holly, from the village of Bacon's Castle. The drive to the house from the road is through a quadruple avenue of old oaks. Bacon's Castle itself stands directly on a smooth expanse of grass. Views of the building from the north and the east are especially reminiscent of Jacobean work in England. Aside from the framing, only a later stair and simple panelled end remain to give interest to the interior.

In Boston, until its demolition in 1922, the Province House (1679) presented a counterpart to Bacon's Castle, being, however, vastly larger in scale and having the remains of six chimney stacks.

Bacon's Castle

THE GABLE END

Cook

BACON'S CASTLE FROM AN OLD PRINT

DETAIL OF WINDOWS | REAR VIEW | DETAIL OF THE EAST CHIMNEY

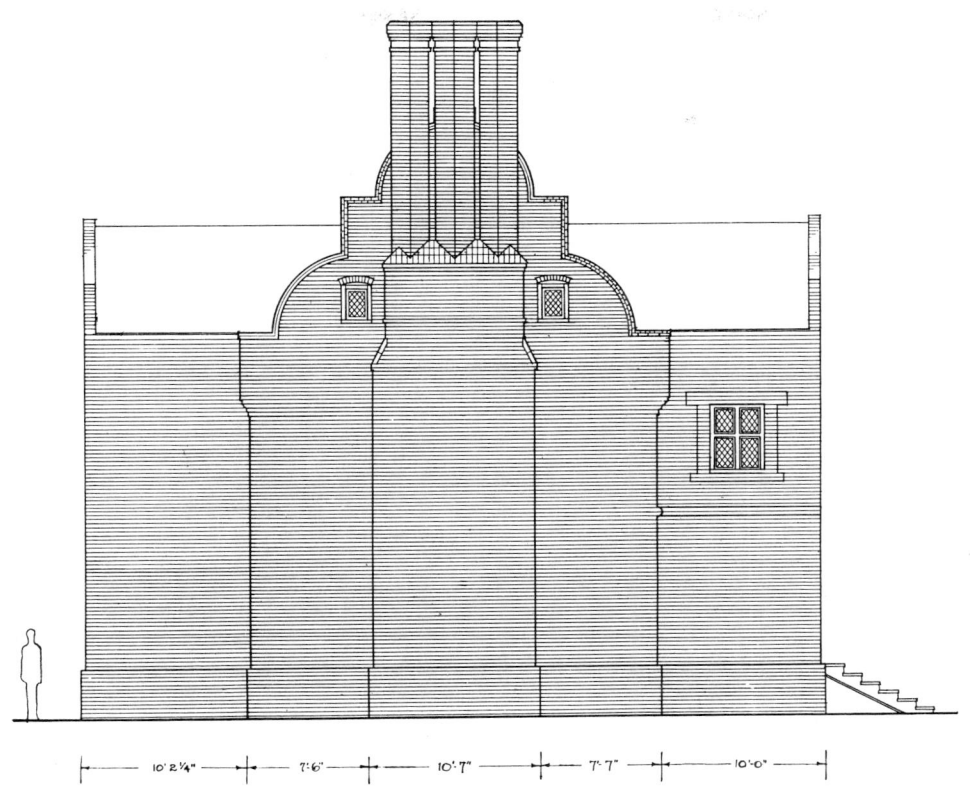

RESTORED WEST ELEVATION

RESTORED SOUTH ELEVATION

Scale, 3/32 in. to the foot

DETAIL OF WEST ELEVATION
Scale, ¼ in. to the foot

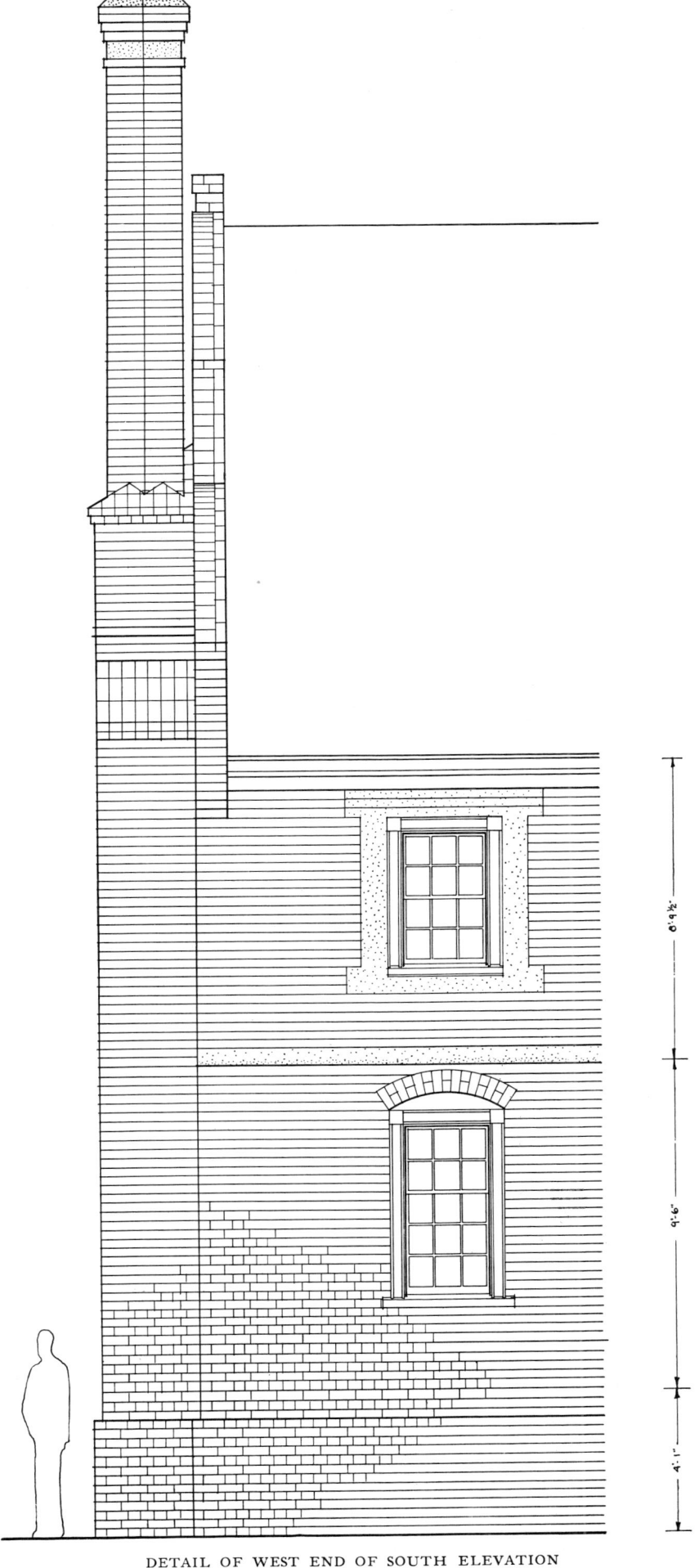

DETAIL OF WEST END OF SOUTH ELEVATION
Scale, ¼ in. to the foot

Fairfield

FAIRFIELD (CARTER'S CREEK PLANTATION HOUSE), NOW DESTROYED, GLOUCESTER COUNTY

Fairfield

GLOUCESTER COUNTY

1692

UPON the vast estate in Gloucester County inherited from his father, Lewis Burwell in 1692 erected Fairfield, once one of the famous houses of Virginia. Its grounds fronted on Carter's Creek, a tributary of the York River, and, according to local tradition, the gardens extended from the house across the intervening fields to the magnificently wooded banks of the creek. Nathaniel, son of Lewis, descended on his mother's side from the Bacons of York County, married Elizabeth, daughter of the great "King" Carter of Corotoman. Their son, builder of Carter's Grove, was President of the Council, and at one time acting Governor of the Colony. The Burwells were descended from an old family of Bedfordshire, England. The immigrant, Major Lewis Burwell, died in Gloucester County in 1658. The fine tombs, recording armorially the family marriages, were removed from the private burying-ground at Fairfield some years ago to Abingdon Churchyard. Very recently the property has been purchased by a descendant of the original owner, and, subsequent to the excavation of the foundation, the house may rise again on the old walls.

The disappearance of none of the great houses of the Colonial Period has been as complete and sudden as that of Fairfield. It stood in much the form in which it was built until about 1900, when it was finally destroyed by fire. At this time the owner permitted the walls to be razed for the brick that was in them, so that now only the foundations remain, covered by trees and undergrowth. Of the once numerous outbuildings only the square floor of a smoke-house, lately destroyed, remains. Near it was found a door, sheathed vertically on the exterior and horizontally on the interior, the two facings being secured together by wrought-iron spikes, arranged in a diagonal pattern. Within a short distance of the house was seen a stone base, of which a profile is here given, together with a fragment of a marble architrave. Fairfield was also known as Carter's Creek Plantation House, from its proximity to Carter's Creek, near which Rosewell also stands.

Without extensive excavations it will be impossible to determine the full extent of the building and the location of the partition walls. The accompanying plan, however, was obtained by diggings at the corners of the foundations and, with the old drawing reproduced herewith, probably definitely establishes the plan as an L. There was found no evidence of a wing, said to have enclosed the court to the south.

Fortunately several photographs exist of the house before the fire, and from these the accompanying restoration was made.

Domestic Colonial Architecture of Tidewater Virginia

The development of the house is difficult to determine, but it would seem very reasonable that the southern end was the original building with one interior and one exterior chimney, as at the Thoroughgood House (1636), Princess Anne County. This may have been flanked by hip-roof dependencies, the north one of which was joined to the main house by a subsequent connection. However, the great length of the house, as it recently stood (80 ft. 6 in. over all), makes it seem unlikely that a further building existed to the south, especially if enough space were allowed to set the main building on axis between the wings. The premise that the middle unit was a connection would explain the curious roof arrangement. That the northern extension or connection was not contemporary may be assumed safely from its different window heights and string-course width. Further, in the photograph, the basement of this part of the building can be seen to have been laid in Flemish bond, while other parts of the existing foundations are laid in English bond.

A SKETCH OF FAIRFIELD MADE BY CHARLES PETERSON FROM AN OLD ILLUSTRATION

Another development may be considered: that the hip-roof building was the original house, and the southern arm comprised two subsequent additions. This is unlikely, as it would relate one chimney, with its double stacks, to each addition—an improbable supposition, since, in the era of change in which Fairfield was built, even ten years would have sufficed to change the design of the chimneys entirely.

The design of the house is important in that it displays the last use of grouped chimney stacks in the colonies, as well as the first

Fairfield

use of three other features: the hip roof, a modillioned cornice, and, possibly, of Flemish bond in a complete building.

The chimneys are the conspicuous features of Fairfield and, in spite of the very great interest of the triple-stack chimney, it is the two on the ridge which are particularly remarkable. They have no counterpart in this country and the type is not common even in England. They are composed of a pair of a wash springs. It would seem that the bricks in the lowest course in the wash were moulded on the outside end and in this case they would probably be laid horizontally with their ends cut to form the wash, as at Province House (1679), Boston, and not perpendicular to the wash as at Bacon's Castle and the Thoroughgood House. The stacks were the usual squares, set diagonally on the base with only their caps engaging. The caps

FAIRFIELD BEFORE THE FIRE, FROM A DRAWING BY W. L. SHEPPARD

stacks on a low base which hardly clears the roof. The cap of this base is enriched by a band of bricks laid so that their corners project diagonally, forming in effect a corbel table for two brick courses above, from which are difficult to analyze from the photograph but would appear to have a projecting course at the bottom of a plaster frieze, a bolder projection of two courses above, with perhaps another narrower plaster band and a final pro-

[33]

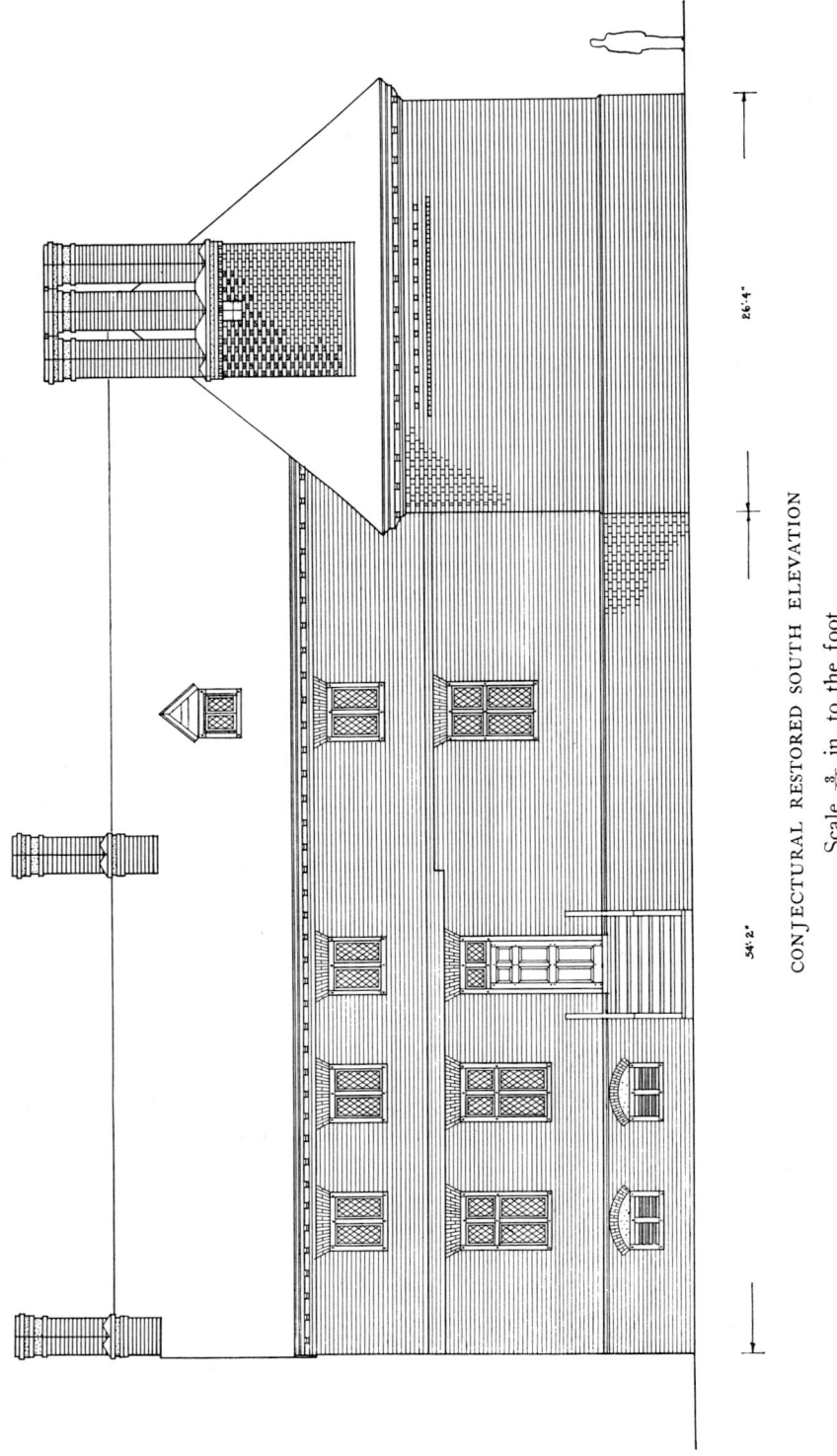

CONJECTURAL RESTORED SOUTH ELEVATION
Scale, 3/32 in. to the foot

Fairfield

jecting course. The detail in the triple chimney is similar, but the stacks are double the height with a base of equal height.

Below the cornice on the wing appears a series of openings or depressions the size of a header, defined two courses below by a course of diagonal projecting brick, the length of the openings above, simulating a dove cote.

Of the exterior woodwork only the cornice and perhaps the dormer on the main roof would seem to be original. The cornice was extremely crude and would appear to be nothing more than a chamfered frieze board against which the brackets were fixed below a cymatium. The modillions seem to have been merely cut to the profile of a double corbel and to have had no moulded capping. The nearest approach to this in Virginia is at the Secretary's Office, Williamsburg, built shortly after 1700. Here the cornice is more sophisticated, having a full bed-mould but the modillions are still undeveloped, being closely spaced ogee brackets.

Nothing can be said about the dormer other than that its unusual proportion might date it as an early example. As has been stated previously, no seventeenth-century dormers are known to be extant. Those appearing on the wing roof may be considered to be nineteenth-century work. A statement that a brick bearing the date 1634 was built in the chimney has never been verified, but it seems to have been authenticated that the date 1692, with the initials "L. A. B.," was used in the decoration of the iron chimney brace.

It is much to be regretted that a transitional house of such outstanding importance should have been destroyed before it could be thoroughly examined. Undoubtedly much will come to light, however, when the foundations are completely excavated.

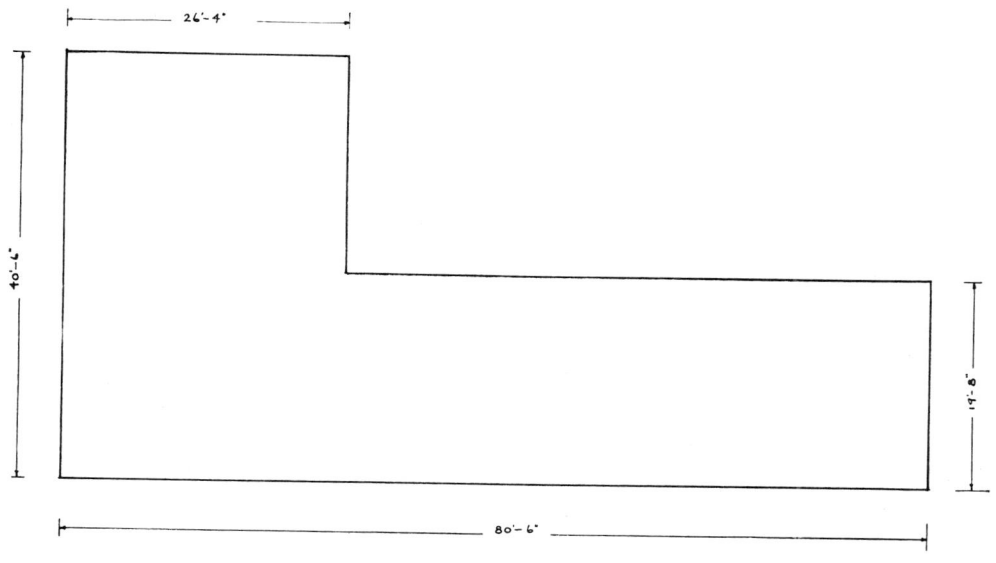

OUTLINE PLAN OF EXISTING FOUNDATIONS

Scale, $\frac{1}{16}$ in. to the foot

Ampthill

Dementi
AMPTHILL ON ITS ORIGINAL SITE

Foster
AMPTHILL AS REBUILT

Ampthill

CHESTERFIELD COUNTY

Before 1732

BETWEEN the years 1695 and 1720 there was much building activity in Williamsburg. Francis Nicholson, Lieutenant-Governor, moved the Capitol from Jamestown in 1699. At that date there stood, in what was then called Middle Plantation, the fine three-story brick college building, a small brick church, several humble frame houses, and possibly a tavern or two. But, with the change of the seat of government, the college suddenly awoke to find itself at the west end of a wide thoroughfare which stretched from its gate eastwardly to land selected for the site of the Capitol.

"Nov. the 9th, 1699, a petition of Mr. Henry Cary to his Excel'cy to be employed to Oversee the Building of the Capitol and by his Exel'cy referred to the consideration of the committee being considered." This is the man, or, as tradition has it, the father of the man who built Ampthill. It is evident that Henry Cary pleased the "committee" for both he and his son superintended the erection of the Governor's Palace and the rebuilding of the Main Building of the College of William and Mary, which was destroyed by fire in 1705. Archibald, son of Henry Cary II, was the most prominent of the family. He was a loyal churchman and in 1770 lent his support in the persecution of the Baptists of Chesterfield County. He was chairman of the Committee of the Virginia Convention of 1776 which met to consider a declaration of rights and plan of government which George Mason of Gunston Hall had drafted.

Ampthill is situated diagonally across the James from Wilton, one of the seats of the Randolphs, and is near the site of the ancient Falling Creek iron works. It is possible that Henry Cary left Williamsburg in 1727 to reopen these works, which were the first in the colony, being established in 1619 but abandoned in 1622 after the great Indian Massacre. It is likely that this adventure proved successful if it were the said Henry Cary who built the present house. It was his son, Archibald, who named the plantation. Mary Randolph of Wilton was his wife, and their names appear in Washington's diary as having entertained the General while he was a visitor in the neighborhood.

There are several very strong arguments against the traditional date of 1732, if the assumption is accepted that Fairfield is the first Flemish-bond house in Virginia. It is said that Ampthill was built by a Henry Cary. If this were the first Henry Cary, it would be the man who superintended the erection of the Capitol and Governor's Palace in Williamsburg. Work on the Capitol was begun in 1701, and it was finished in 1705. Cary was then ordered to "oversee" the erec-

Domestic Colonial Architecture of Tidewater Virginia

tion of the "Governor's House" which was begun in the same year the Capitol was completed. Both buildings were in accordance with the latest styles, and were of brick in Flemish bond. Remaining masonry shows a salmon-colored brick and glazed headers which in color are not unlike the Brafferton and the President's House at the College of William and Mary, and Bruton Parish Church. If it were this Cary who built Ampthill house, it would have been, without doubt, a Flemish-bond building, unless he had erected it before 1692, when Fairfield was built. The latter is the first authenticated Flemish-bond building in America, the date being given by iron figures in the gable, accompanied by the initials of Lewis and Abigail Burwell, the then owners. It does not seem plausible if Cary built his house after 1700 that he should follow a style which at the Capital was out of vogue. If Henry Cary the elder did erect the dwelling, it must have been before 1701, the date when foundations of the Capitol were laid, for the amount of work he superintended in Williamsburg covered roughly a period from 1701 until 1730. The College building postdates Fairfield but three years. It is an English-bond building, but inasmuch as Pembroke (1701?), Nansemond County, is Flemish bond and the earliest remaining brick buildings in Williamsburg are of the same pattern, it is very likely that the former is the last of the English-bond structures.

The supposition that the second Henry Cary was builder of Ampthill is even more difficult to authenticate than the former. This Cary, with his father, was also superintendent of the Governor's Palace. It was he who built the President's House in 1732, the same year that Ampthill is said to have been erected. This, in itself, is not reasonable; the President's House was not finished until the following year, and Mr. Cary probably was required to devote his entire time in Williamsburg. If it were this second Henry Cary who was the builder, why should he erect this house in English bond when Bruton Church (1715), the Powder Horn (c. 1715), the Brafferton (1723), the Chapel of the College (1732)—all after the Capitol and the Palace—were erected in Flemish bond?

Local Jacobean characteristics are in evidence at Ampthill. They are: first, the plan; second, the glazed-head string course; third, the English-bond brickwork. The panelling and the dependencies no doubt date from 1750 to 1760, inasmuch as Wilton (1754) repeats many of the same mouldings used in Ampthill interior. Archibald Cary, son of Henry Cary II, probably made these alterations, and it is likely that the dependencies were built at this time, being laid in Flemish bond and having much the character of Wilton. Perhaps the builder of Wilton was employed on the remodelling of Archibald Cary's house.

From the archæological point of view, Ampthill is perhaps the most interesting house in Virginia. The accompanying roof diagram indicates the several stages through which the building passed before its present form was attained, and all shed light on its existing plans and elevations. As it stands today, the front of the central building boasts

Ampthill

AMPTHILL BEFORE REMOVAL

of no more architectural importance than a rather heavy cornice of both modillions and dentils, and a string course laid in Flemish bond with glazed headers. This latter detail is employed in the string course of the Thoroughgood house (1636), Princess Anne County, and, granting the date 1732 authentic, it is the only example of glazed-head string courses in major architecture of the eighteenth century in Virginia.

The window jambs on both first and second floors have the minimum dressings, as well as the corners of the house. The water-table is only a bevelled, rubbed brick. The flat arches on the first floor are a header and stretcher high and those of the second are but a stretcher high. The segmental arches of the basement are rubbed stretchers with false joints in alternate bricks, simulating headers. The segmental arch is characteristic of the seventeenth-century work, but also appears in the first quarter of the eighteenth century in the basements of great houses, as at Westover (1726), Charles City County, and Stratford (1725–30), Westmoreland County. All of the brickwork of the main house is laid in English bond.

The development of the main block of Ampthill is most clearly followed in the roof framing. No. 1 (page 44) shows the form of the first roof which spanned the building, the full length and half the depth of the present house. The chimneys were apparently exposed on the rear wall, as clapboarded gables

Domestic Colonial Architecture of Tidewater Virginia

DEPENDENCY BEFORE REMOVAL

are still extant filling the spandrel between them and the returned gables. That the latter exist rather indicates that the completion of a U-shaped plan was contemplated. This fact alone is indicative of an early date, as no such plan seems to have been used in Virginia after 1701, the date of the erection of Pembroke, Nansemond County, except at Elsing Green, King William County, built in 1754. The framing of two hips abutting these gables, as well as joints in the brickwork of the side elevations, clearly shows that the U-plan was actually completed at a later date. Plan No. 2 refers to this development, and No. 3 shows the third hip that was finally added to enclose the impracticable narrow court formed between the two wings. That this stage was reached before the close of the Georgian Period may be confirmed by examination of the woodwork in the hall that the later addition provided. The joints in the brickwork of the rear wall, as well as a change in plane of over six inches between the projection of the old wings, now filled by a diagonal wall, further authenticates this fact. The arrangement of the triple roof, so common in England, must have proved impracticable here, as, in almost contemporary framing, a low hip was superimposed on the ridges of the other roofs and the three rear hips were joined to form a continuous surface. The use of round-end shingles in the Georgian Period was unexpectedly verified by finding *in situ* shingles of this design on

Ampthill

the courtyard slopes of the roof which had been covered continuously from the date of the final addition.

The dependencies which flank the central house are built on line with the front of the main building. They are low-hipped, one-story, brick structures, standing well above the grade, with large segmental windows to ventilate the space below the water-table. Their composition is simple; a large central door, flanked by two windows on the front, with chimneys in each building built inside of the end wall farthest from the main house. The cornices are enriched by modillions, and the jambs of the windows and the corners of the houses are simply rubbed. The brick below the water-table is English bond and not gauged, except the arches of the openings and the impost bricks upon which they are received. Above the floor line the bonding becomes Flemish. There are no glazed bricks in the buildings.

In 1928 the property was purchased as a site for a large commercial development, as the location had become unsuitable for residential purpose, and the house was removed and rebuilt in Richmond by descendants of the brother of the original builder. As is shown in the photographs, the windows of both the main building and the dependencies

REAR OF THE MAIN HOUSE

DETAIL OF BRICKWORK OF THE MAIN HOUSE

Domestic Colonial Architecture of Tidewater Virginia

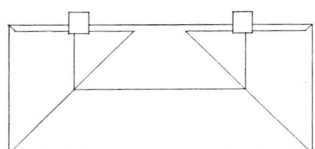

1. Hip roof with temporary gables to take future wing roofs

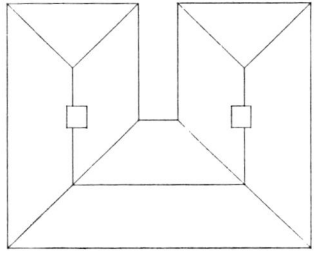

2. Wings added, forming court, and hips continued from temporary gables

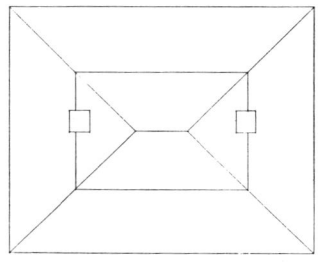

3. Court eliminated and space covered by another hip

4. Three hips covered by continuous roof forming hip on hip

DEVELOPMENT OF ROOF PLAN

RESTORED END ELEVATION
Scale, $\tfrac{3}{32}$ in. to the foot

[44]

Ampthill

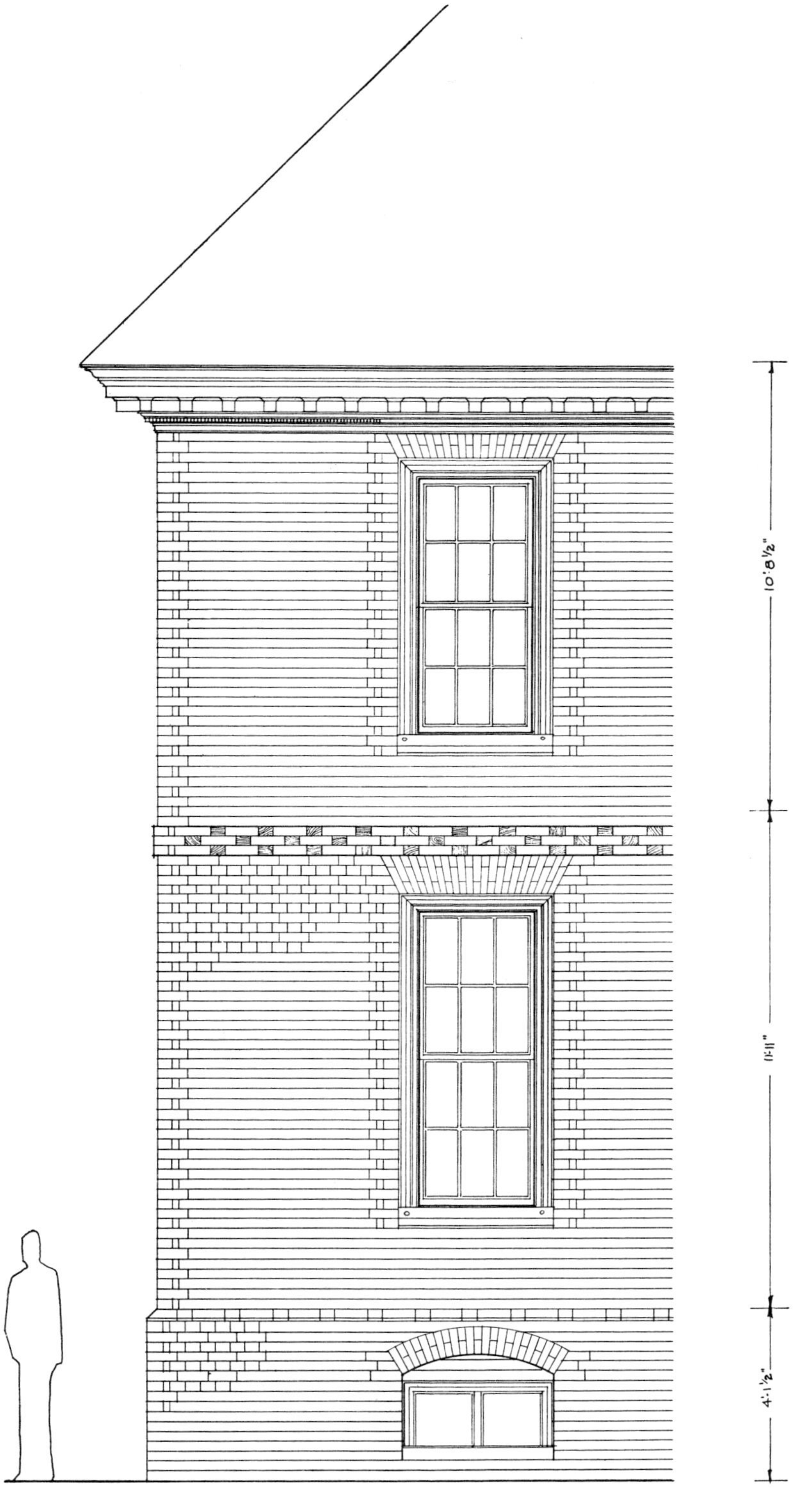

DETAIL OF FRONT ELEVATION

Scale, ¼ in. to the foot

[45]

Ampt

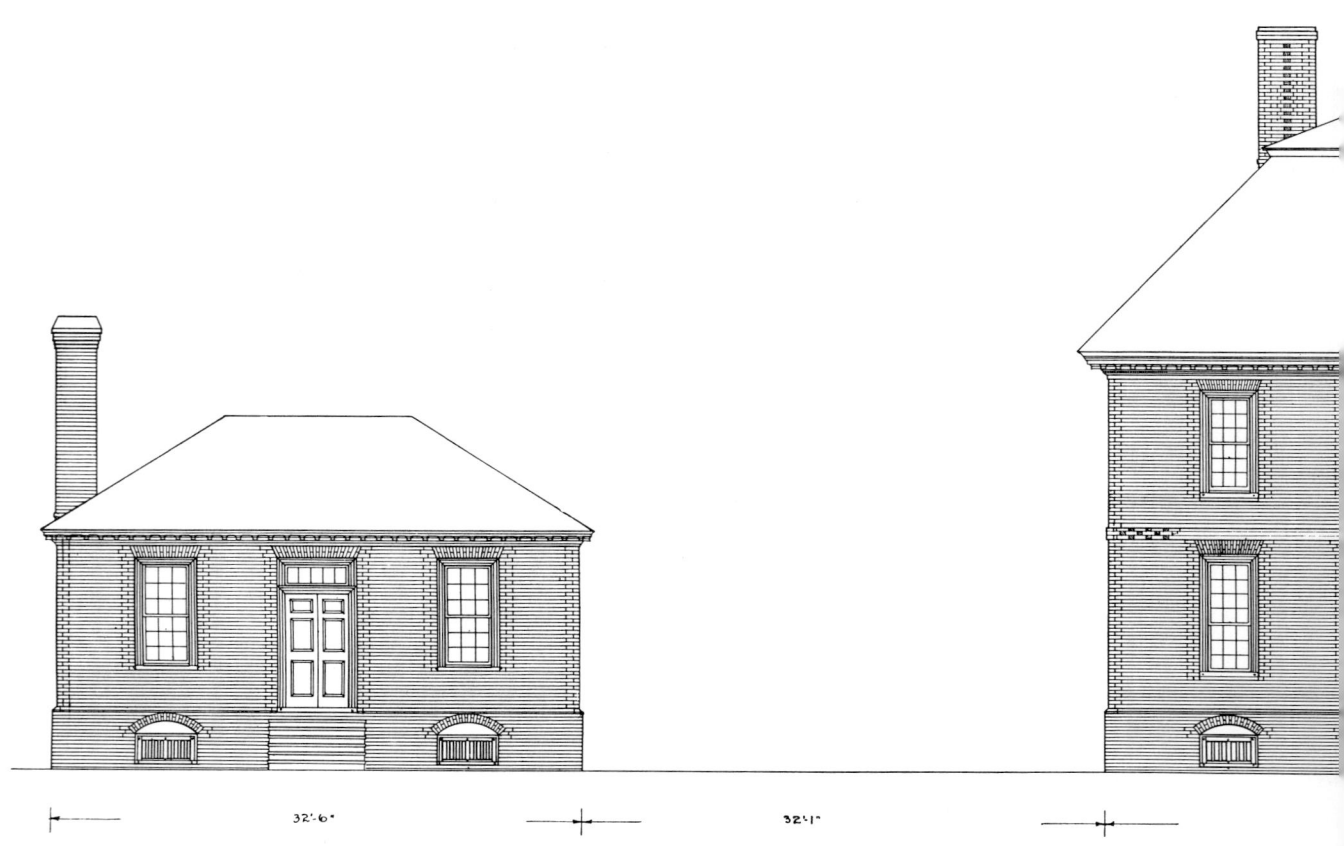

RESTORED FRONT EL
Scale, $\frac{3}{32}$ in. to th

Domestic Colonial Architecture of Tidewater Virginia

were boarded for protection. A modern porch covered the front door, and an unpretentious addition of considerable age had been erected on the right end of the building.

Some fragments of panelled stonework were found near the front porch and elsewhere about the property. It is possible that these may be Georgian steps similar to those in place before the doorway of the Archibald Blair house (1718), Williamsburg.

The detail here presented is of a corner of the front of the house. The sash indicated is that which was in place behind the protective boarding. In the restoration, conjectural Georgian sash take the place of the later glazing.

The President's House

THE PRESIDENT'S HOUSE, COLLEGE OF WILLIAM AND MARY, WILLIAMSBURG

The President's House

COLLEGE OF WILLIAM AND MARY, WILLIAMSBURG

1732

THE President's House and Brafferton Hall form the north and south sides of the forecourt of the Main Building of the College of William and Mary. Early drawings indicate that the details of the design of both buildings were similar. Thus the President's House is substantially a replica of the Brafferton, although built nine years later. By date of design it is representative of the earliest type of Georgian dwelling in Virginia. The northern elevation has escaped material alteration and has for this reason been chosen for presentation rather than either elevation of Brafferton Hall.

The College of William and Mary received its Royal Charter in 1693. An entry in the Executive Journal of the Council of Virginia, dated July 25, 1695, states: ". . . that the Committee had Appointed Thursday the Eighth of August next for the laying of the Foundation of the Said College and prayed his Excellencys Company at that time."

The tradition that Sir Christopher Wren was the architect of the Main Building has never been substantiated. Mr. Thomas Hadley came over from England as surveyor of the building. The paragraph in Jones's "Present State of Virginia," 1724, which states: "the building is beautiful and commodious, being first modelled by Sir Christopher Wren," gives rise to the Wren tradition.

Brafferton Hall was built for the Indian school by funds derived from the Brafferton estate in England. The date 1723 is carved in a brick near a door of the building, and further substantiated by a line in Jones's "Present State of Virginia," which reads: "As there has lately been built an Apartment for the Indian Boys & their Master . . ." Indians were educated at the College before the erection of Brafferton Hall, however, for in an item dated July 23, 1700, we read: "this next Summer the rooms will be made ready at the College for their reception & accomodation & if any one Great Nation will send 3 or 4 of their children thither, they shall have good, valuable clothes, books & learning & shall be well look'd after both in health & sickness & when they are good scholars, shall be sent back to teach the same things to their own people."

The President's House was erected in 1732. On June 28 of that year the College Chapel was opened, and a letter from Reverend William Dawson to the Bishop of London, dated August 11, 1732, states: "The foundations of a common brick House for the President was laid opposite to Brafferton." The Reverend Mr. Blair was at that time president of the College and he, "Mr.

NORTH FRONT OF THE PRESIDENT'S HOUSE

The President's House

Fry, Mr. Stith, and Mr. Fox" laid "the first five bricks in order, one after another." Mr. Henry Cary, son of the builder of the Capitol was the "Undertaker" or superintendent of the work.

In 1781 it was occupied by the French officers and, during their occupancy, was accidentally burned. Louis XVI, it is said, rebuilt the house with moneys taken from his private exchequer. The walls fortunately were not harmed; in fact, the extent of the damage is unknown. The only definite indication of later work on the exterior is the use of undercut modillions in the cornice, a feature unfamiliar at the date of the erection of the house.

The brickwork is especially noteworthy, both in color and elaboration. The walls are laid up in Flemish bond, the stretchers being a soft salmon color, and the headers covered with a silver gray glaze. The arches and jambs of the windows, the string course, and corners of the building, are rubbed brick of a bright vermilion color, emphasizing the architectural features of the structure. The windows are wide, but, being divided into four lights rather than the customary three, create a distinct vertical character which is further emphasized by the dormers occurring over the piers, the steep sweep of the roof, and the location of the T-shaped chimney stacks at the end of the ridge.

The use of the floating pediment, with the exception of those formerly over the doors of the Brafferton building, is unique in Virginia. The character of the moulding indicates it to antedate the fire of 1781. It is a feature that adds interest to the otherwise simple façade.

The fact that it is placed against the string course might have proven awkward had it not been that the transom of the door was carried up to line with the arches of the flanking window. The jointing of the brick in the arch above the door is richer than that of the arches of the windows. The elaboration of the window arches themselves varies with the importance of the floors. Those in the segmental head of the basement windows are the simplest, and those of the second floor follow next in importance.

The sash on the first and second floors probably dates from 1781, but possibly may be original. The dormers, however, from the character of their detail, are obviously subsequent to 1800.

A conspicuous feature of the house is the entrance stair and wrought-iron rail. Each step, and the platform as well, is a monolith of gray-veined marble. The risers and ends are tooled vertically, with wide bands of horizontal tooling at the corners. The rail is light and graceful and terminates in a swirl on an octagonal newel. The use of marble here is unusual, Portland stone from England and native Aquia Creek stone being the customary materials for exterior architectural detail.

In the drawing presented herewith only the door itself and the grilles in the basement windows are conjectural restorations. The tympanum below the segmental arch is of plaster as at the Warren House, Surry County. The grilles are according to local Williamsburg precedent. The existing slate roof is modern, and replaces a former shingle roof. Little of interest remains within the house, due to a recent fire.

Domestic Colonial Architecture of Tidewater Virginia

DETAIL OF THE DOORWAY

WEST SIDE

DETAIL OF WINDOW

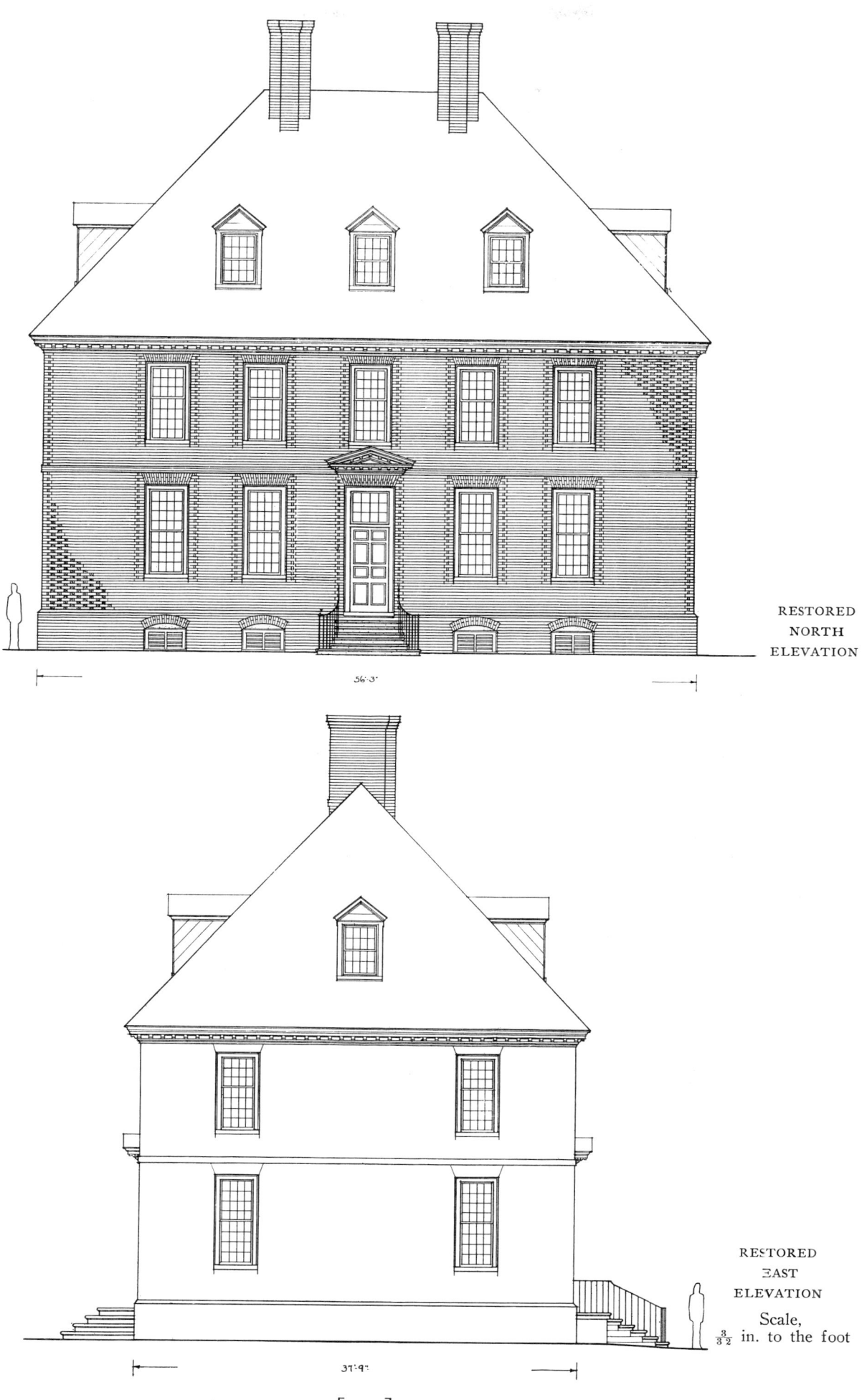

RESTORED NORTH ELEVATION

RESTORED EAST ELEVATION

Scale, $\tfrac{3}{32}$ in. to the foot

Domestic Colonial Architecture of Tidewater Virginia

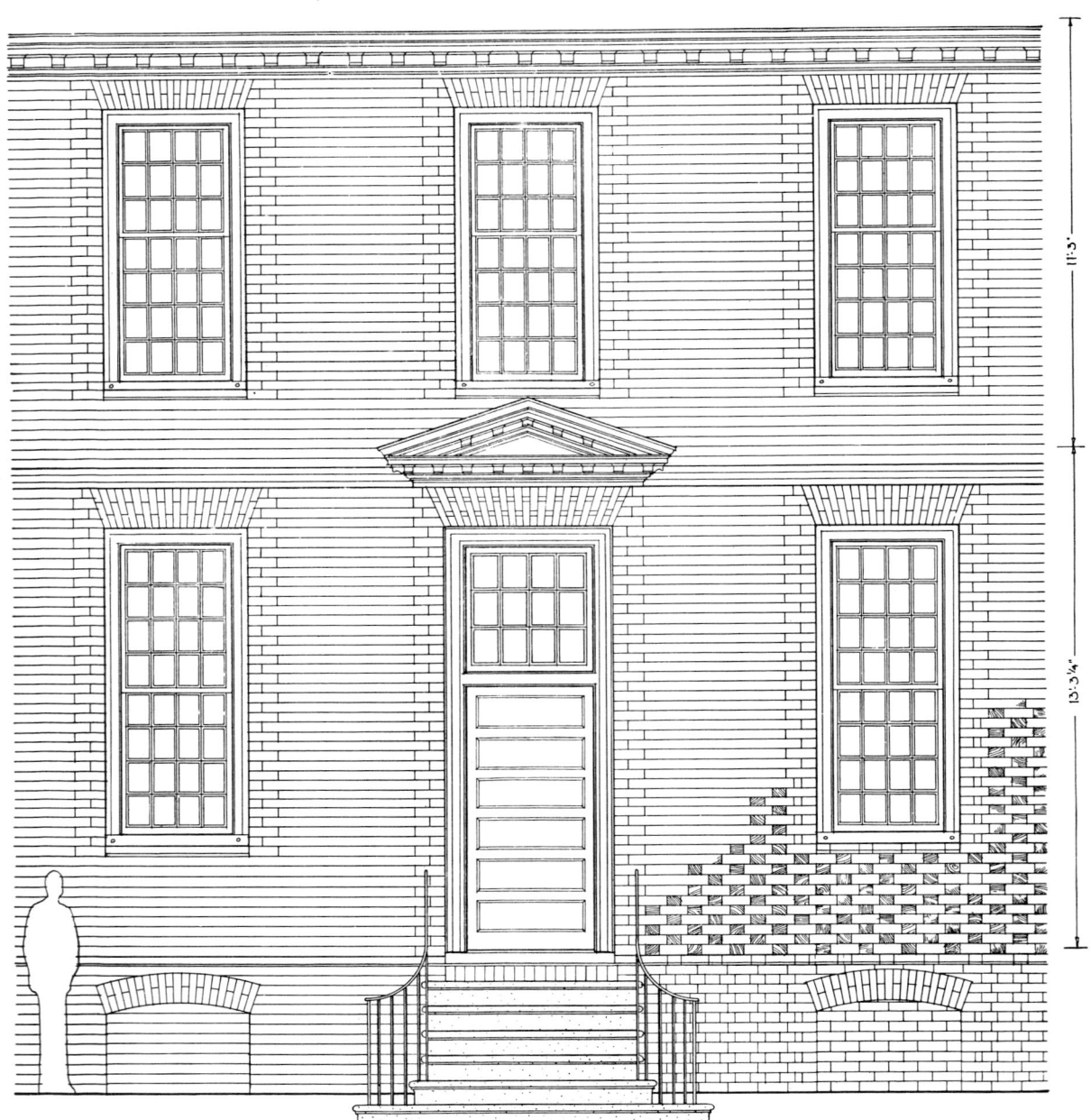

DETAIL OF NORTH ELEVATION
(THE DOOR IS MODERN)
Scale, ¼ in. to the foot

Stratford

STRATFORD, WESTMORELAND COUNTY

Stratford

WESTMORELAND COUNTY

Between 1725 and 1730

STRATFORD was built between the years 1725 and 1730 by Colonel Thomas Lee, a man of influence and power in Westmoreland County. He served not only as local magistrate, but also as President of the Council, and later as Acting Governor of the Colony. His wife was Hannah Ludwell of Greenspring—one-time residence of Governor Berkeley. The widow of the latter married Colonel Phillip Ludwell of Rich Neck. Thus Greenspring came into the possession of the Ludwell family, from whom it went to the Lees, who were responsible for its demolition.

Thomas Lee was the father of six sons, four of whom were born at Stratford. They were: Phillip Ludwell Lee, who became a member of the House of Burgesses and was secretary of the Council; Thomas Ludwell Lee, also a member of the House of Burgesses and later a member of the Committee of Safety and of the Convention of 1775; Richard Henry Lee and Francis Lightfoot Lee, both signers of the Declaration of Independence; and William and Arthur Lee, both of whom served in the diplomatic service in Europe during the Revolution. Robert E. Lee and Fitzhugh Lee, both great generals, were of a collateral line, the former having been born at Stratford.

Richard Lee, of Stratford-Langton in Essex, England, came to Virginia in 1644. He settled first in Gloucester County on an estate named Paradise, and was the grandfather of Thomas Lee, the builder of Stratford. This great house has, in all probability, given more famous men to the nation than any other in America. It was the home of twelve members of the House of Burgesses, four of the King's Council, four of the Convention of 1776, and two signers of the Declaration of Independence. It gave governors to Virginia, and members to the Continental Congress, and was the birthplace of one of the greatest military geniuses the world has ever known.

Life at Stratford must have been very picturesque. Fithian, the Samuel Pepys of the Rappahannock and Potomac regions, mentions the house in his diary. His entries throw much color on affairs of the times. He describes dancing classes, even to the extent of just who danced the minuet and how well he or she performed.

The last of the Lees to own Stratford was Major Henry Lee. At his death, which occurred in Paris in 1837, Stratford was acquired by his sister-in-law, Mrs. Starke, and by her was bequeathed to her husband's nephew, Doctor Richard Stuart. His son, Charles Edward Stuart, has recently sold

Domestic Colonial Architecture of Tidewater Virginia

it to the Robert E. Lee Memorial Foundation, who propose to restore it, and make it, like Mount Vernon, a national shrine.

The main house with its subsidiary buildings forms a *parti* which in completeness is not rivalled in Virginia. The plan of the house is an H, found elsewhere in the State at Tuckahoe (1710–30), Goochland County. The two outbuildings which flank the house, twenty-eight feet in advance of it, are of early character, with gable roofs clipped at the end walls. The rear dependencies are placed in a similar relation to the main house, but are much more in the style of the house itself, with hip roofs and level cornices.

The brickwork of the front dependencies is similar. In both, door and window openings have segmental heads and have simple dressings. The cornices of the advance buildings are inconspicuous and are received at the corners by end boards. The roofs are unbroken except by tall chimneys, which in design carry out the feeling of those of the main house. Here the flues are accentuated by little panels which terminate with an arch, approximately at the base of the caps. The brickwork in the chimneys is similar to that in the walls. The corners are rubbed, as are the caps. In effect these buildings, with their low walls, high unbroken roofs, and clipped gables, are distinctly foreign.

The house is surmounted by a low, unbroken hip roof. The first floor is built but a step above the grade and in the design is treated frankly as a basement. The windows are low and have segmental heads, a characteristic basement treatment. Above them is an elaborate and unusual water-table which defines the principal floor as being the upper one. The main doorway of the house is on this level. At the head of a long flight of stone steps, one enters the salon, which fills the arm of the H. Opening from it out of narrow transverse halls are the other major rooms. The windows on this floor are large, and the ceilings high.

Below the water-table the walls are laid up in Flemish bond with glazed headers. The size of the brick here is greater than that above. The width of the joint is also larger. This difference, coupled with the effect obtained by the use of glazed headers, creates a horizontal coloring across the base of the house which is both interesting and unusual.

Although the basement windows are the same width as the first-floor openings, the latter are increased in scale by very elaborate rubbed dressings, and their formality is emphasized by flat arched heads in contrast to the segmental heads of the basement openings.

The brickwork above the water-table is well laid with narrow joints, and the brick itself is unusually regular in size. Though of Flemish bond like the walls of the lower floor, no glazed headers are employed and the coloring, due to this and to the narrowness of the jointing, is a bright red.

Both corners and window jambs of this floor have rich dressings. The rubbed brick in each case reaches the maximum. The flat arches are gauged, and in height they consist of a header, closer and stretcher, and the reverse, the sophistication of which differs greatly from the simple treatment of the first-floor openings.

Stratford

Stratford, like Rosewell (1720–30), Gloucester County, and Carter's Grove (1751), James City County, has architectural door frames of gauged and moulded brick. The treatment on each front is practically identical and, though interesting, is

REAR DEPENDENCY

not to be compared to the magnificent brick detail at Rosewell and the quieter but scholarly designs at Carter's Grove. The piers flanking the doors are flush with the flat arch, which is surmounted by a truncated pediment. The mouldings are crude and are not unlike provincial Jacobean work in England.

It is the chimney stacks at Stratford which make the design of the house practically unique. Four flues from the rooms in each wing carry in independent stacks above the roof and are united by semi-circular arches just under the cap. In the space thus enclosed a gazebo is created, the platform of which, by windows in its vertical surfaces, forms a clerestory to light the space under the roof. A heavy cornice-cap is above the arched opening and breaks out about the stacks themselves. It is made up of variations of the same mouldings employed in the water-table and doorways. It has all the elements of a

Stratf[ord]

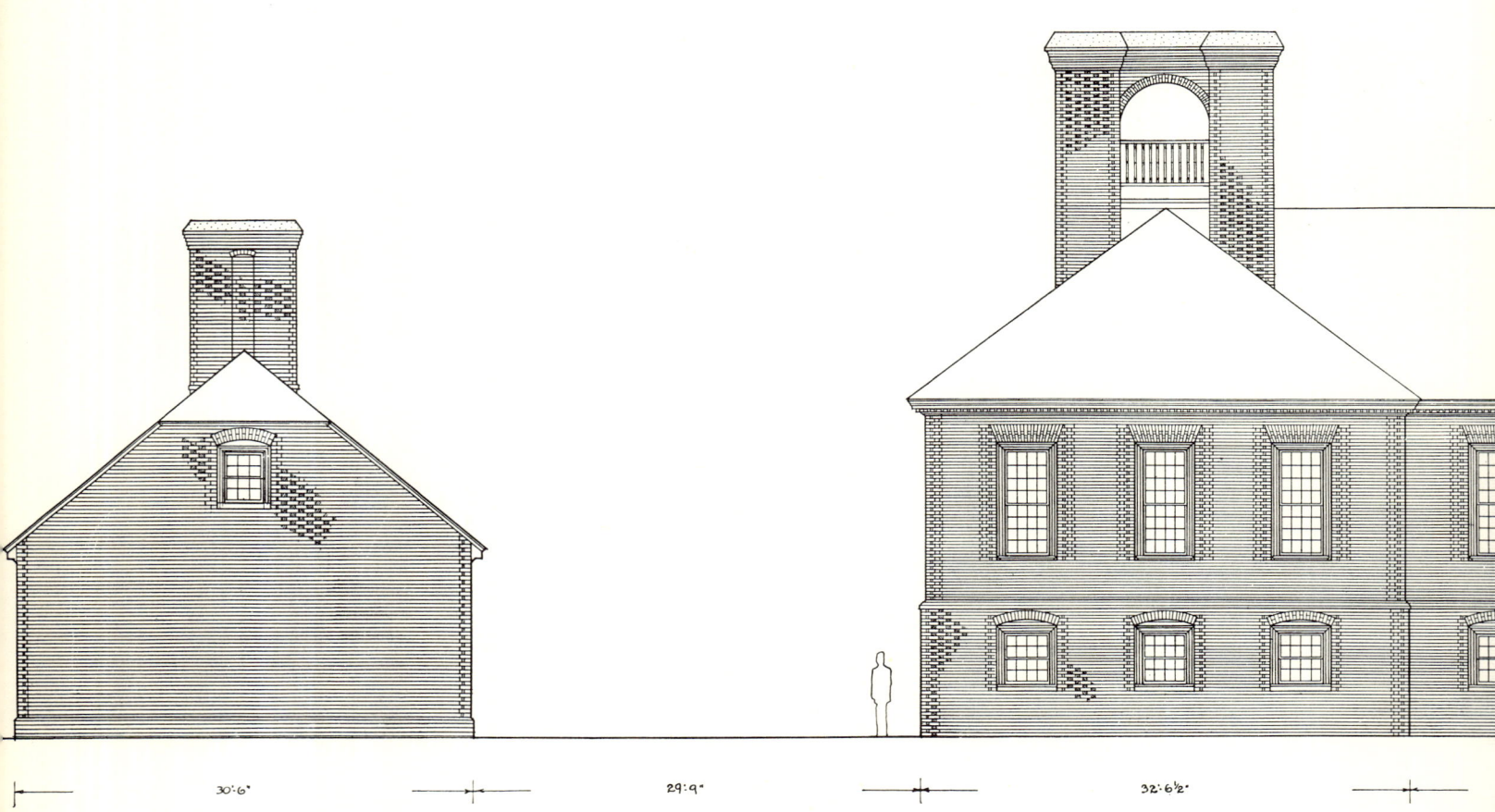

RESTORED SOUTH ELEVA[TION]
Scale, $\tfrac{3}{32}$ in. to the fo[ot]

DETAIL OF DOORWAY

DETAIL OF CHIMNEY

Stratford

full cornice, comprising eight courses in all, and is surmounted by a plaster wash, the equivalent of four additional courses. The crown of the cap is, together with the torus in the water-table at Carter's Grove, a rare example of a moulding made up of two courses of brick. Glazed headers reappear in the stacks and carry up to the bottom of the cap. The corners of the chimneys are rubbed, and the omission of glazing in the spandrels simulates gauging. The white of the plaster wash forms a very effective top to the composition. A light wood rail between the stacks completes the design.

The side elevations of the house are simple. A central door is flanked on either side by two windows, that of the east front being reached from the ground by a long flight of stone steps, guarded by an iron rail. Unfortunately, the original entrances were altered by an addition of early nineteenth-century porches. The doors themselves are of that date. A semi-circular transom replaces the former Georgian motive.

In design, the cornice of Stratford differs from that of any other Georgian house. It consists of the conventional crown and bed-mould, but the modillions are no more than large dentils which reach out the full projection of the soffit of the cymatium. The effect from the ground is quite good and seems in scale with the low hip roof. The frames of the second-floor windows may well be considered original. The sash, however, would seem to date from the early nineteenth century. Much old work was removed at that time, the salon being one of the few remaining Georgian rooms in the building. The frames of the basement windows also seem to be original, but the width of the muntins indicates the sash to be of a later date. The glass size is far more convincing than that used in the larger openings. In the accompanying restoration, it was used as a basis for the new lights above.

The detail here presented shows half of the projecting wing of the house as it exists. The dimensions are from the ground to the top of the water-table, and to the bottom of the cornice, floor heights not being obtainable.

The unusual elevation of the main floor of the house from the grade may be traced to the influence of Lord Burlington's Palladian school, expressed in Chiswick Villa. It is said that the present Stratford was built after the burning of Thomas Lee's first home at Mount Pleasant. The latter was burned by convict servants who had been sentenced to be punished by Colonel Lee, magistrate of the County. In appreciation of the loss sustained from this disaster, the English Crown gave financial assistance in building the present house. This close relation between Stratford and England might explain the Palladian influence found here. With the exception of the vanished gardens and the addition of the small side porches, Stratford stands in very much the same form as when erected. The group of buildings that surround it is very complete. Even the brick barn, a contemporary structure, remains, the yard of which is screened from the house by a high brick wall.

Strat

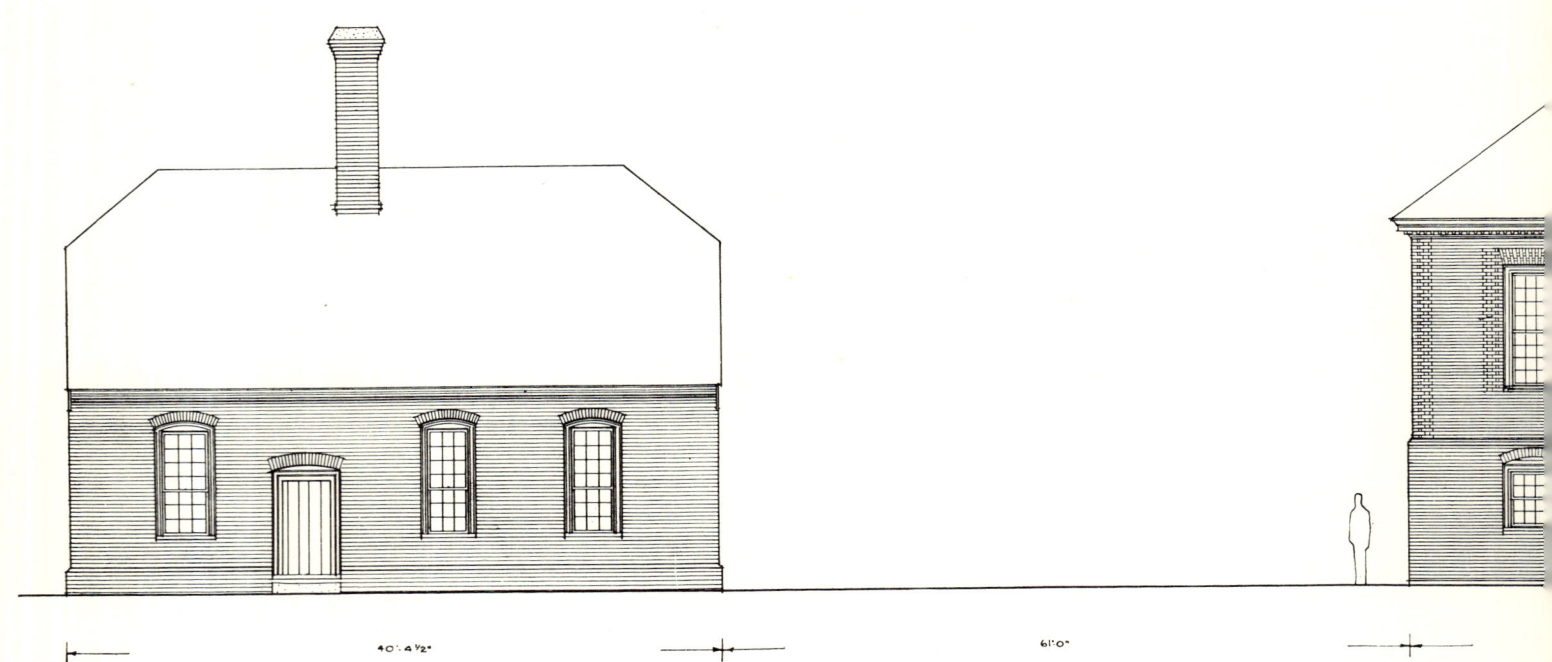

RESTORED EAST EL
Scale, $\frac{3}{32}$ in. to th

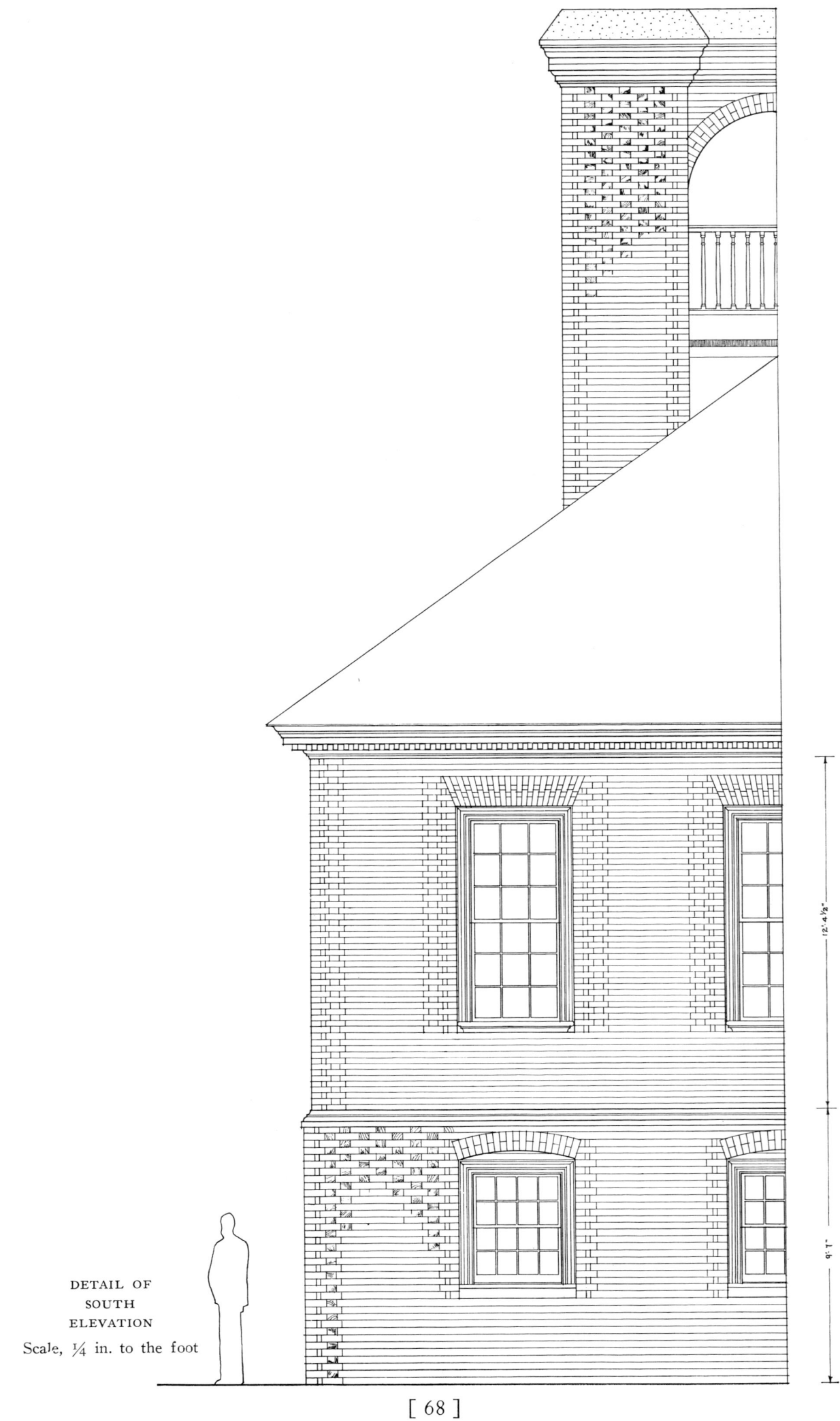

DETAIL OF
SOUTH
ELEVATION

Scale, ¼ in. to the foot

Westover

WESTOVER, THE SOUTH FRONT, CHARLES CITY COUNTY

Westover

CHARLES CITY COUNTY

1726

THE land upon which Westover is built was patented by Thomas Paulett, January 15, 1631. From its earliest days it has been known by the same name, for it is said that it was first called Westover by Thomas Paulett in honor of Captain Francis West, brother of Lord de la Warre. The plantation was laid out by Sir John Paulett, brother of the patentee, who in turn sold it to William Byrd I, in 1688.

This ancestor of the Virginia Byrds came to the colony about 1673 to claim several large patents of land that were willed him by his uncle, Captain Thomas Stegge. The outcome of the Civil War in England had been distressing to Stegge and, like many of his station, dismayed at England under the rule of Cromwell, he migrated to Virginia, where, not long afterward, he died.

Byrd was the son of a London goldsmith. His wife, who came to Virginia with him, was Mary, daughter of Colonel Warham Horsmanden of Kent. They took up life at Belvedere, the house of Thomas Stegge, which was at the "Falls," where the present city of Richmond now stands. It was there that William Byrd II, was born March 28, 1674. He became one of the great men of the colony. He was the builder of the present Westover house, was owner of the largest library in Colonial Virginia, the catalogue of which lists 3,625 volumes, and he was the author of the famous Westover Manuscripts, comprising "The History of the Dividing line betwixt Virginia and North Carolina," "A Journey to the Land of Eden" and "A Progress to the Mines," as well as the founder of Richmond and Petersburg. He held innumerable colonial offices. The inscription on his tomb tells us that ". . . he was made Receiver General of his Majesty's revenues here, was thrice appointed to the Court and ministry of England, and being thirty-seven years a member at last became President of the Council of this Colony."

In 1706 he married Lucy, daughter of Daniel Parke, whose eldest daughter, Frances, the year before had become the bride of Colonel John Custis, ancestor of Martha Washington's first husband. Byrd's second wife was Maria Taylor of Kensington, England. He was the father of six children: Evelyn, the famous beauty; Wilhelmina, who married Thomas Chamberlayne; Anne, who became the bride of Charles Carter of Cleve; Maria, who wed Landon Carter of Sabine Hall; Jane, who married John Page of North End; and William, who was next to the youngest of the family, and who inherited Westover.

The story of Evelyn Byrd is well known. She went to England when but eighteen and

Domestic Colonial Architecture of Tidewater Virginia

was presented at Court. It was there that she met Charles Mordaunt, Earl of Peterborough, who fell in love with her and to whom she became engaged. William Byrd was not pleased at this turn of affairs, the Earl being a Roman Catholic and he a stanch Episcopalian. He therefore hurried his beautiful daughter back to Westover. After her forced return to the James she had many suitors; among them, Daniel Parke Custis, favored by her father. He, however, married Martha Dandridge, who later became the bride of George Washington. William Byrd wrote to the Earl of Orrery, to whom he had "attracted a most close and bosom friendship" while in England for his education: "Either our young Fellows are not smart eno' for her, or she seems too smart for them." His conscience apparently did not hurt him because of the spinsterhood of his eldest daughter, who died unmarried, it is said of a broken heart. The portrait of Charles Mordaunt, suitor of the beautiful Evelyn, to-day hangs in Carter's Grove.

Upon the death of William Byrd II, his son, William III, inherited the estate. During the French and Indian War, when Washington was a colonel of one of the two regiments of the Virginia militia, this William Byrd commanded the other. Thus it was that the two formed a close friendship, that proved later to be one of the steps toward the end of the unfortunate last Byrd owner of Westover.

William III was a most prodigious gambler, and unfortunately his luck was almost always against him. His father said that he gambled "as fashionable amusement merely." This "fashionable amusement," however, cost him many acres of land and at the death of his wife Westover was sold for his debts.

When the storm cloud of the Revolution broke in all its fury upon the colonies, this same man remained true to his King. His sons, who were in England, returned to Virginia—one to fight for England, the other to fight with Washington. It was the disloyalty of this great friend to the Crown, coupled with that of his own son, and perhaps the weight of the tremendous debts that were ever oppressing him, that led him to take his life. The house remained in the family until the death in 1814 of his second wife, Mary Willing of Philadelphia.

It is interesting to note that, during the war, Benedict Arnold landed at Westover and set out from there with over nine hundred men bound for the destruction of the town that the second owner of the mansion had founded.

The personality of this second owner of Westover is the personality that the house expresses to-day. The fine panels within were hung with a superb collection of portraits. The furniture was the best of the period, and even the marble mantel in the drawing room was imported from Europe. Outside, the same personality was expressed. The stone doorways, the magnificent iron gates, the boxwood gardens, the position of the house itself, all tend to create an atmosphere that is unexcelled in the country. The formality of the north front, the symmetrical placing of the buildings, the great trees, the ivy-covered garden walls, all give color to the present—color that speaks vividly of the past.

Westover

Cook

FROM THE RIVER

The clairvoyée before the north front of Westover is the only existing example in Virginia. Its presence not only lends unusual interest to the design, but unites the group into one composition. Entrance to the enclosure is gained through a gateway enriched by an elaborate wrought-iron overthrow, in the scroll work of which appears the cypher of the builder of the house. This, with the simple iron gates, is supported by heavy plaster-covered piers with delicate stone caps. Great stone balls are placed hereon, and poised on them, facing the house, are finials in the shape of large birds. This, and the smaller garden gateways, are the finest examples of English ironwork in America. A series of carved stone finials, on plaster-covered piers, defines the flanking bays of the clairvoyée. In all probability these bays were intended to be filled with wrought iron, but whether this elaborate scheme was fulfilled or not is unknown. Until recent years, however, a heavy wooden picket fence, supported on a low brick wall of no more than three or four courses in height, served the purpose. To-day, a modern cast-iron fence has been substituted.

In design the finials are varied and interesting and were without doubt carved in England. The material appears to be Portland stone, as are the steps and the stone door trim of both fronts of the house. The accompanying photographs convey some idea of the richness of the carving of the many designs.

The façade of the main house is probably better known than that of any Georgian

WESTOVER, THE NORTH FRONT

Westover

building in America. Both fronts are practically identical, with the exception of the doorways. The north one, strangely enough, the finer both in proportion and detail, is not as famous as the more baroque south entrance with its broken pediment and carved stone pineapple. The central doorways, in each case, are reached by extremely wide stone steps of pyramidal form. Flanking the entrance are three windows with segmental heads, which recur with slightly smaller dimensions on the second floor. The tops of the arches are cut off by the bed-mould of the very delicate dentilled and modillioned cornice. An exceedingly high roof, pierced by five dormers on the longitudinal fronts and by one between the stacks at each end, rises above the house to a height nearly equal to the distance between the top of the water-table and the bottom of the cornice. Above the third floor is a fourth floor or attic, which is lighted by a scuttle on the south slope of the roof. The framing is probably original with the house and is unusually fine. Kingposts rest on a timber apparently supported by the longitudinal partition wall. From these, braces are framed to the main rafters. The material used is of large scantling and is nicely pinned together in characteristic eighteenth-century manner.

The roof is covered with graduated slate. The texture is rough and the variegated sizes and irregular shapes would indicate that it is not a modern covering. If this proves to be a fact, Westover may safely be cited as a rare example of original slating. The roof of the original gabled dependency is also of slate and is laid in a similar manner.

A contemporary painting shows the Westover group as it appeared during the Civil War. There are certain architectural errors, such as the Palladian motive over the door. The painting is interesting, however, in that it definitely establishes the design of the burned dependency to be similar to that of the remaining one. The roof is a gable and there are two end chimneys. There are also a central door and two windows. Because of the existence of the modern building it was impossible to determine the size or exact location of the former. In the accompanying restoration the original dependency is duplicated in size and position.

The segmental windows of the main house are unique. The design is even repeated in the basement, which, in form, is a characteristic seventeenth-century treatment, but at Westover the frame follows the line of the arch as it does on the upper floors. The brick below the water-table is English bond, but above becomes Flemish. The corners, window jambs and string course are rubbed. The water-table of two courses, a cove and ovolo, is gauged. The basement window arches are simple, being only one course in height, with joints scratched on intermediate bricks to imitate a half brick. Those of the first floor are of stretcher, closer and header, and the reverse, in order, and those of the second floor are of header and stretcher. The dressing about the window is the minimum and carries down to the top of the brick wash below the moulded sills.

The north door is a scholarly design, completely executed in stone. Traditionally it is said to have been imported from England and

Domestic Colonial Architecture of Tidewater Virginia

its sophistication would substantiate this. The opening is surrounded by a stone architrave which is flanked by excellently proportioned Corinthian pilasters. The fluting of the shafts, the moulded bases, and the carved capitals are representative of the best English work of this period. The pilasters are surmounted by a segmental pediment with carved modillions above a full entablature. The south door is similar, but the order used here is Composite. The frieze is pulvinated. A broken serpentine pediment with coarse carved terminal rosettes encloses a pineapple finial. The delicate enriched modillions of the north door are here replaced by heavy double moulded brackets. The effect of this door is less satisfactory than the other, due to its clumsy detail.

The fenestration of the side of the house is very similar to that of Wilton (1754), Henrico County. On either side of the two chimneys are grouped windows, and though at Wilton these openings are narrower than the others in the house, at Westover they are the same size. Due to the height of the roof, the stacks at Westover are very tall. They are laid up in common bond and now have moulded caps of metal.

In comparatively recent years there was much painting done on the brickwork of the main house. The foundation to the water-table line is white, as is the string course. The south front was painted dark red. Happily this has weathered somewhat and the color of the joints is again beginning to show.

The remaining old dependency is very interesting. Its character is as horizontal as the main house is vertical. The floor is but a step above the ground, while the cornice is hardly above the line of the meeting-rail of the mansion's first-floor windows. The roof is very steep, pierced on the south front by three dormers and at the ends by large square chimneys. Their caps are unusual, consisting of a necking of one course, surmounted by a flat plaster band about three courses in height, topped by three additional courses which corbel out and are then brought back to the line of the shaft by a plaster wash. One crowning course completes the caps.

An interesting detail in connection with the chimneys is the fact that at neither end of the dependency are they bonded into the walls themselves. The total projection is but three inches and the profile of the shaft is further accentuated by the unbroken joint that carries along the sides of the stacks. The design of the chimneys is strikingly like that of the Thoroughgood House (1636), Princess Anne County, and it is easy to believe that these may have been the stacks of an earlier frame building, possibly the residence of the first William Byrd. At all events, it is clear that these chimneys antedate the walls.

There is no gauged brick employed in this building save in the segmental arches over both windows and doors. In each case the arches are stretcher, closer and header high, laid with as great a degree of skill as those in the main house. The brick here is smaller and of a different color and texture than that of the mansion and, like it, is laid in Flemish bond. However, occasional glazed headers are used.

In the accompanying drawing the modern dependency and both connections were

Westover

omitted. The metal caps on the chimneys of the main house were replaced by a simple design of brick. As several of the sash, frames and basement grilles are original, no further restoration was necessary. The colonnaded connection, though extremely interesting and satisfactory, has every appearance of being an early nineteenth-century intrusion, and, for this reason, has been omitted. In detail the north door shows the relation of the stonework to the window openings. The brickwork, on both fronts, between the pilasters and the jambs of the windows, bears indications of having been disturbed. It is said that Westover was partially burned during the christening of William Byrd III, and these stone features may have been installed during the rebuilding, however extensive this may have been.

The situation of Westover is delightful. The south façade is shaded by tremendous tulip poplars, and under these, paralleling the house, is a narrow gravel path leading on right and left through boxwood walks to beautiful wrought-iron gateways in the ivy-covered garden walls. Near the river's edge are several of the Westover tombs, while in the quaint old-fashioned garden is the shaft erected over the remains of the builder of the house.

Courtesy of The Century Association, New York. Photograph by D. MacDonald-Millar
WESTOVER, FROM THE SOUTHWEST, AFTER THE PAINTING BY E. L. HENRY IN 1863

Courtesy of the Virginia State Chamber of Commerce

WESTOVER FROM THE RIVER

Westover

PIERS AND GATES

DETAIL OF SCREEN

PIER AND VASE

MINOR PIER AND FINIAL

RESTORED NORTH EL[EVATION]

Scale, $\frac{3}{32}$ in. to the [foot]

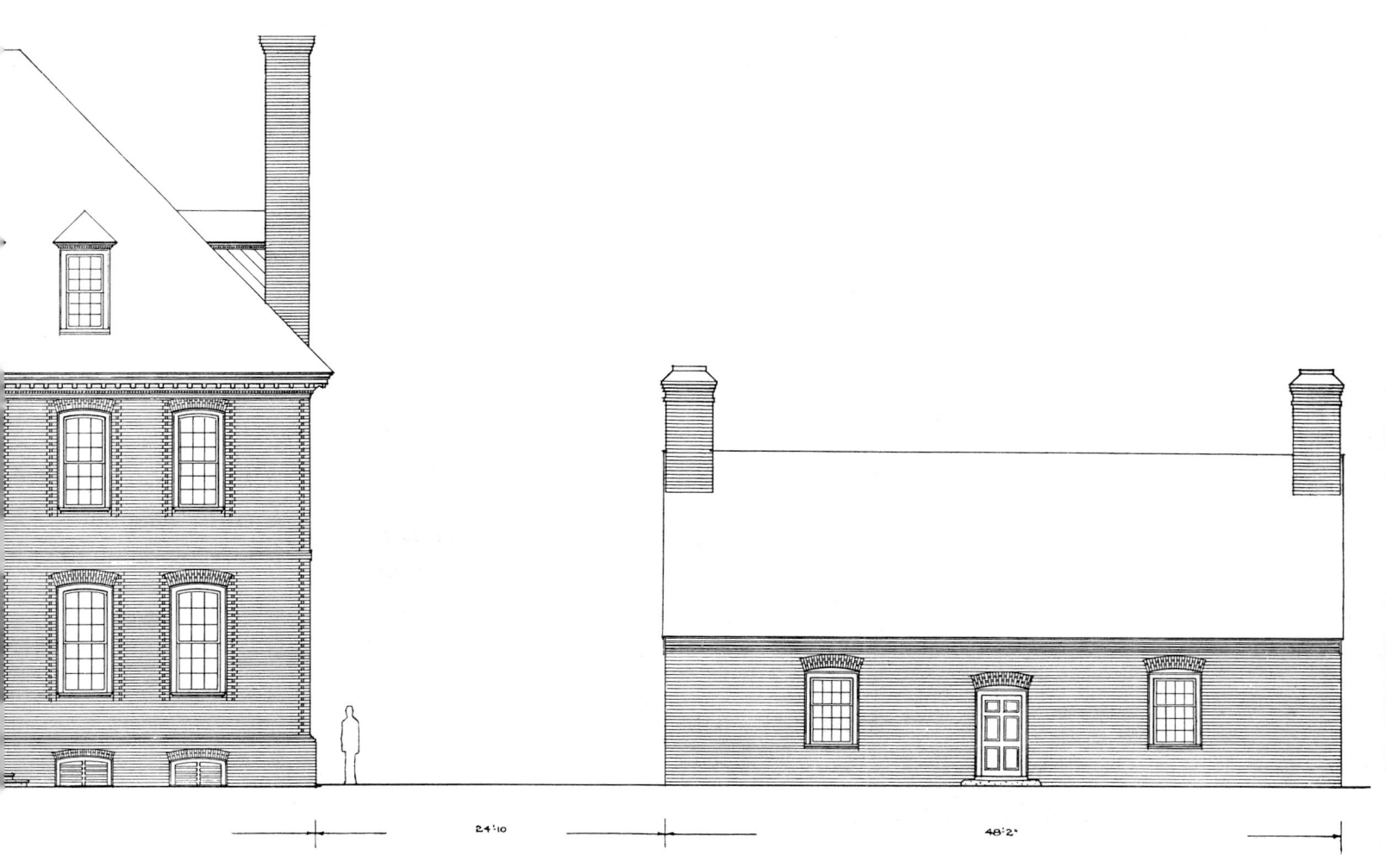

Domestic Colonial Architecture of Tidewater Virginia

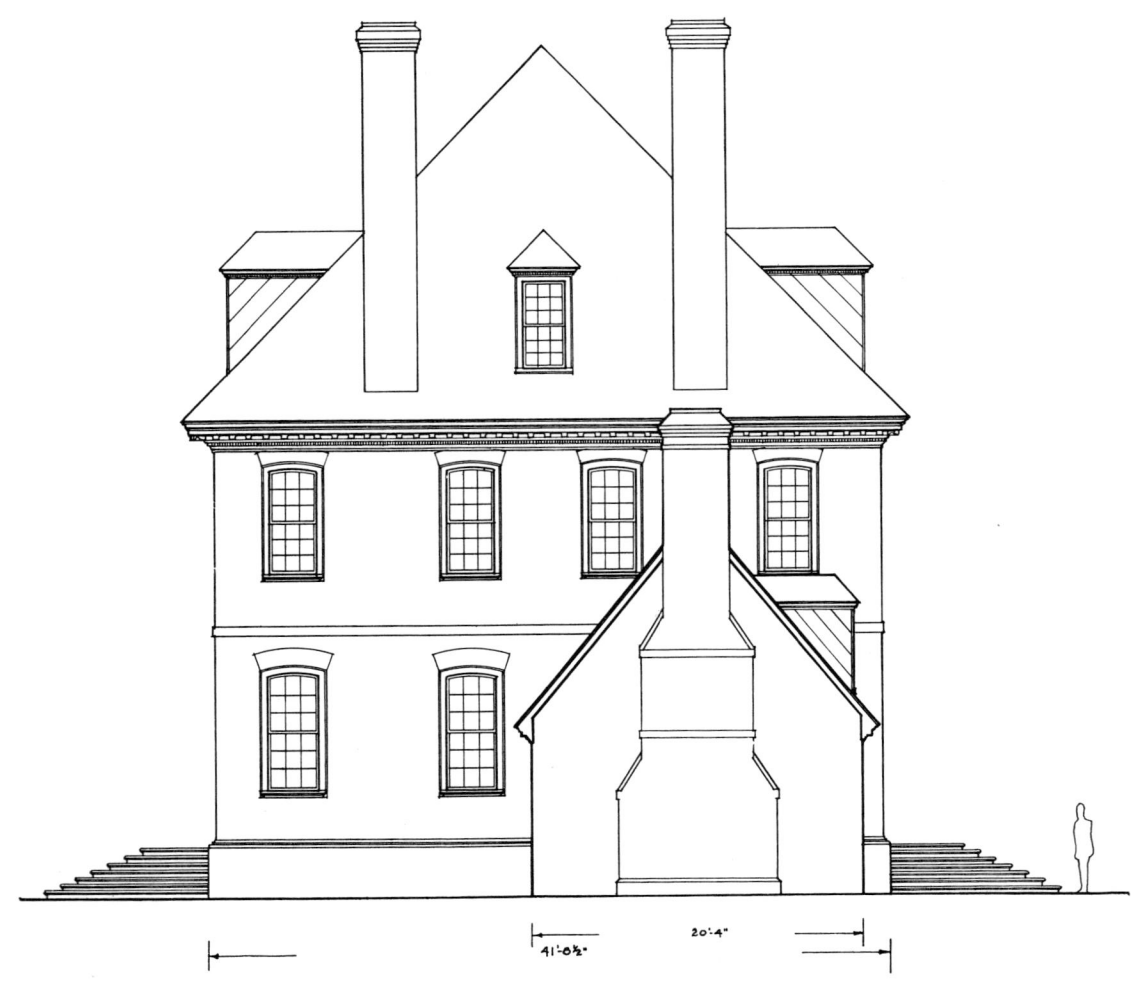

RESTORED WEST ELEVATION

Scale, $\tfrac{3}{32}$ in. to the foot

Westover

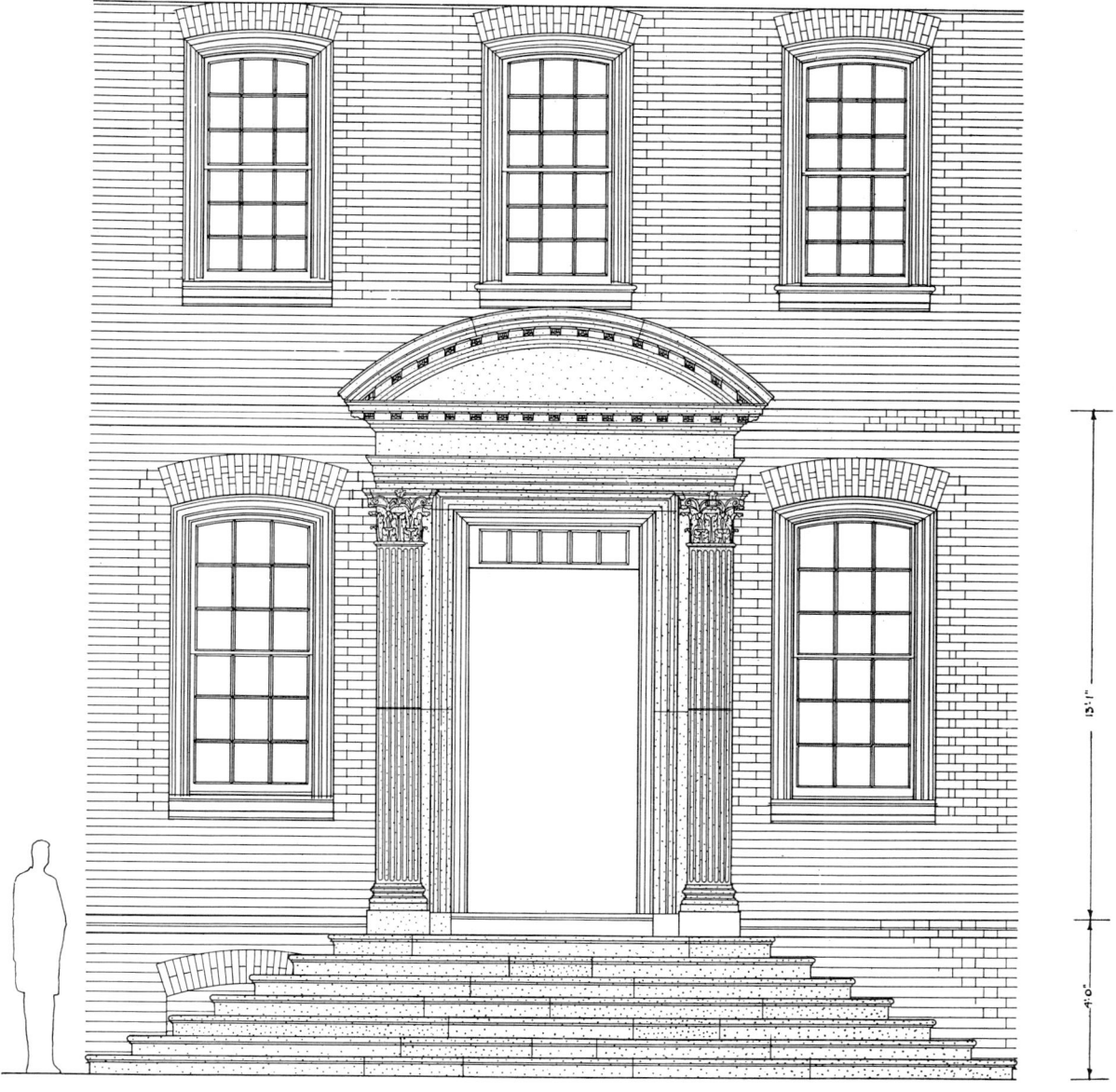

DETAIL OF NORTH ELEVATION

Scale, ¼ in. to the foot

Rosewell

ROSEWELL, GLOUCESTER COUNTY

Rosewell

GLOUCESTER COUNTY

Between 1720 and 1730

THE estate of Rosewell, on the York River in Gloucester County, was identified with the Page family from the seventeenth to the nineteenth century. In 1692 it was bequeathed by John Page, first of the family in Virginia, to his son Matthew Page, whose tomb still stands in the family burying-ground at Rosewell beside that of his son, the builder of the great house. The dwelling of Matthew Page and Mary Mann, his wife, was an unpretentious frame house. Inspired perhaps by the building of the Governor's Palace in Williamsburg, and perhaps by Westover and Stratford, Mann Page set out to house himself in a suitable mansion, but died in 1725, leaving it for his son Mann Page II to complete. The expense of building this vast house was so great that the heir found it necessary to apply to the Assembly to break the entail, enabling him to sell lands to pay for the work already completed. The property enumerated as sold for this purpose comprised over twenty-seven thousand acres in various counties in Virginia. The house was finally completed, however, and its interior contained some of the most magnificent woodwork in the colonies, including a superb stairway that survived until the fire of 1916.

John Page, born at Rosewell in 1744, was a close friend of Thomas Jefferson. The two corresponded continually through their college days, and it is a tradition that Jefferson came to Rosewell and read the Declaration of Independence to Page in the seclusion of one of the cupolas on the roof before it was submitted to Congress. Page was the only member of Lord Dunmore's Council in 1775 who refused to sign the proclamation censuring Patrick Henry for his activities in retaliation for Dunmore's seizure of the powder in the Williamsburg magazine. He was a member of the Committee of Safety appointed in 1775 to take charge of the executive functions of the colony, and was a member of the first council under the Virginia constitution of 1776. Page was also active in the campaign on the peninsula against Benedict Arnold. After the Revolution he was a member of Congress from 1789 to 1797, and in 1802 was elected Governor of Virginia.

Rosewell might be called the climax of Georgian architecture in the colonies, if it were not for the fact that it antedates most of the other great houses of the style and is contemporary with those that it does not antedate. The only known earlier eighteenth-century mansion in Virginia was the Governor's Palace in Williamsburg, 1705, which was burned in 1781. The plan of Rosewell is possibly a development of that of the Palace, a measured drawing of which is preserved among Thomas Jefferson's papers. There is little similarity between the two elevations, however, the latter more resembling Westover. An engraving of the Palace, of which no representation had hitherto been known,

Domestic Colonial Architecture of Tidewater Virginia

was recently discovered by an American research worker in England. This shows a deck on hip roof, similar to that indicated on the accompanying restoration of Rosewell, though lacking the parapet and possessing dormers. About 1835 the parapet, cupolas and roof of Rosewell were replaced in the current style and, like Blandfield (1760), Essex County, the panelling was completely removed, though, unlike it, the doors and stairs were permitted to remain. The destruction was completed in 1916, when the house was burned, but the brick walls stand as the finest specimen of brickwork of the Colonial Period. When the dependencies were removed is unknown.

Much adverse criticism has been made of the design of Rosewell, but the building as it stood before the fire little resembled the original structure. In the restoration here given an attempt has been made to complete the missing parts of the fabric in order to give the main house its proper context.

The walls as they stand now are reasonably complete to the underside of the cornice, although small sections weakened by the fire have given away. It is three full stories, standing upon a basement six feet high. The plan is a square with projecting pavilions on the side elevations, avoiding the boxiness that is so apparent at Shirley, Charles City County. As is customary the forecourt is on the land side and the foundations of one of its terminal buildings are still discernible. The floors of the house are expressed by an elaborate water-table at the line of the first floor, and by moulded string courses at the second and third floors. The front is five windows wide, the openings over the entrance being two lights wider than the typical window. Flemish bond is used for the entire exterior of the building, with random glazed headers. It may be that the glazing was once consistent, as at the President's House (1732), Williamsburg, and that the surface has disintegrated, but this is unlikely.

Up to the date of the building of Rosewell, rubbed brickwork was sparingly used. At the Main Building of the College of William and Mary (1695), in Williamsburg, the arches, belt courses, window jambs and corners were only simply rubbed, and this is also the case at Westover (1726), but at Stratford (1725–30), Westmoreland County, and at Rosewell the maximum, or dressings a header, closer and stretcher wide, suddenly occurs. It is possible that the Capitol (1701) in Williamsburg, now destroyed, and the Governor's Palace are the transitional examples that are missing. Not only are the arches, jambs, belt courses and corners of Rosewell rubbed, but also the elaborate doorways and aprons below the windows. All of these features, except the jamb and corner brick are not only rubbed but also gauged. The window aprons connect the color of the window dressings and definitely unite the windows into tiers, which gives the building the vertical accent that the mass requires.

The water-table is the most sophisticated in Colonial architecture, simulating the profile of a balustrade. It is three courses high, a torus supported on a facia, coved at the top to take a filet, and surmounted by a very flat cyma. The offset, taken between the basement and the wall of the superstructure, is

Rosewell

W. H. T. Squires

A VIEW OF ROSEWELL FROM THE SOUTHEAST

W. H. T. Squires

A VIEW OF ROSEWELL FROM THE NORTH

nearly three inches. The water-table runs completely around the house, breaking out under the windows to receive the projecting aprons. These have but slight relief and are capped by moulded stone windowsills. The jambs of the openings are of alternating courses of rubbed brick; a header, closer and stretcher wide, and a stretcher and header wide. The flat window arches are cut to a segment on the soffit with the horizontal joints of the arch conforming to this shape. These arches have elaborate stone keys, fluted and with moulded caps. They are received in the brick arch by stone lugs cut to the size of the abutting brick voussoirs. This arch is typical even in the basement openings except on the third floor where no caps exist. The great arched windows that formerly lighted the stair halls have a variant of the typical keystones: an awkward wedge, five flutes wide, the outer ones being shortened to allow a curious scroll above them. These round arches rest on moulded imposts.

Both string courses are five gauged courses high, the lowest member, all headers, being moulded, a cyma in one case and an ovolo in the other. The flat member is consistently laid in Flemish bond.

The two doorways are entirely in gauged brick, moulded, cut and carved, and are the most elaborate pieces of brickwork in America. They even vie with the craftsmanship in such houses at Tyttenhanger and the Cromwell house in England. The north doorway is the better design, but has suffered very greatly from the fire. In the accompanying detail drawing the fallen pediment has been restored, from the section of it remaining over the right corbel. The door was framed by a moulded brick architrave of three members, eared on the sides at the top. The architrave is flanked by moulded pilaster shafts that spring from stone bases and support narrow, boldly projecting brackets which are moulded on the edge and carved with elementary scrolls on their return faces. Although the brackets corbel out fifteen inches, they return in a large scroll to the face of the wall, obviating the necessity of supporting the pediment. A pulvinated frieze runs between the brackets and takes the cornice of the pediment, which, in itself, is composed of seven moulded courses including a denticulated band which also occurs on the rake. A cyma caps the rake but it is not carried across the horizontal cornice. The true pediment thus formed is one of the earliest in the Colonies. In the débris under this doorway was found a section of what may be presumed to have been the wood jamb moulding. This is square on two sides, rebated on the third and run with a bolection moulding on the fourth. No other example of this type of moulding is known to exist in this country. The stone steps were removed many years ago and may be seen in fragments nearby. The curved stones for the terminal swirl are used to cope a spring wall. An incised line was found on the brickwork under the doorway and is shown on the detail drawing. This probably indicated the width of the steps.

The South doorway is heavier and less dextrous in design than the North. Pilasters flank the opening, with coarse stone caps and bases of a pseudo-Doric order. The shafts are of brick, carved with flutes. At one time these were covered with cement, the flutes being visible only in places. The pilasters support a clumsy architrave, surmounted by a pulvinated frieze. The architrave, where it carries over the door, has fallen. A segmental pediment, less rich in detail than the North pediment but still denticulated, caps the composition.

The four truncated chimneys remain, with their huge stone cornices. Built in the shafts are the fragments of the original parapet coping. The entire chimney shaft above the parapet seems to be of rubbed brick.

All of the projecting architectural features of the building are flashed with lead as at the Main Building of the College of William and Mary and Carter's Grove.

The restoration presented here is largely supported by the walls themselves and by literary evidence; some points, however, are conjectural. The photograph showed sash of an obviously late date, with the possible exception of that in the third floor. This was arched to conform to the segmental window heads but had no trim other than a staff bead. Christ Church (1731), Lancaster County, and Menokin (1769), Richmond County, have this same feature, but in early building the dimension from the brick jamb to the clear opening usually varies from six to eight inches. The wide trim is used in this restoration. The cornice is entirely an assumption, that in the old photograph being, on close examination, of the neo-Classic period. This, together with the careless bonding of the pavilion pediments, which fell in the fire, would place them as innovations of the nineteenth century. The continuous parapet is substantiated by a description of the house before the alteration, written in 1876, which also describes the two cupolas,* shown together with the level parapet by Bishop Meade. The flat roof shown in his engraving may have been occasioned by the foreshortening of a deck on hip such as is shown in the restoration and as is known to have

*"Leonora and the Ghost." Baltimore, Charles Harvey & Co., Printers, Cor. South & German Streets: 1876:—
"It was called Rosewell from an abundant spring near which the house was built.
". . . A wall of bricks, surmounted by large flagstones, surrounded the top of the building. At each end was a tur-

Rosewell

existed at the Governor's Palace. A door filling the entire opening of the main entrance is still in position at Carter's Grove and would seem to be reasonable at Rosewell, since the hall was adequately lighted by several windows, making a transom unnecessary. The type of the exterior stair is determined, but no evidence exists for the iron rail. Racking remains around the two side doors, indicating that connections were contemplated, and while descriptions mention them, no evidence can be found to show that they were ever built. Those shown here are similar in plan and arrangement to those at Mount Airy (1758), Richmond County. The location of the western dependency was determined at the site, but no information as to its design can be found other than that in the old photograph. The walls are seen here to be laid in English bond, which at Rosewell is only used for interior walls, making the assumption reasonable that the fabric of the building underwent changes. Two-story dependencies are found at Mount Airy, Blandfield, Shirley, Brandon, and Menokin.

Even in its ruined state Rosewell contains unique structural features of the Colonial Period that are of greatest importance and which are well worthy of exhaustive research. In addition to the main house, several superb early sculptured tombs, an old circular ice-house, and traces of the garden remain to afford material for study. The mansion is rapidly falling into complete ruin.

ret, within which were small apartments, and on the roof of each, large weather cocks whirled mournfully. Into one of the rooms you ascended from the winding staircase, leading from the basement to the roof. From the other, called the summer house, you beheld from its four fine windows beautiful views of the winding Carter's Creek, and the majestic York River.

"An immense floor of lead, with wide gutters to let off the melting snow, or falling rain, was much admired by visitors and it was asserted in 'Howe's History of Virginia' that Governor P. and his friend Thomas Jefferson caught fish up there."

ROSEWELL FROM AN ENGRAVING IN BISHOP MEADE'S "OLD CHURCHES, MINISTERS AND FAMILIES OF VIRGINIA"

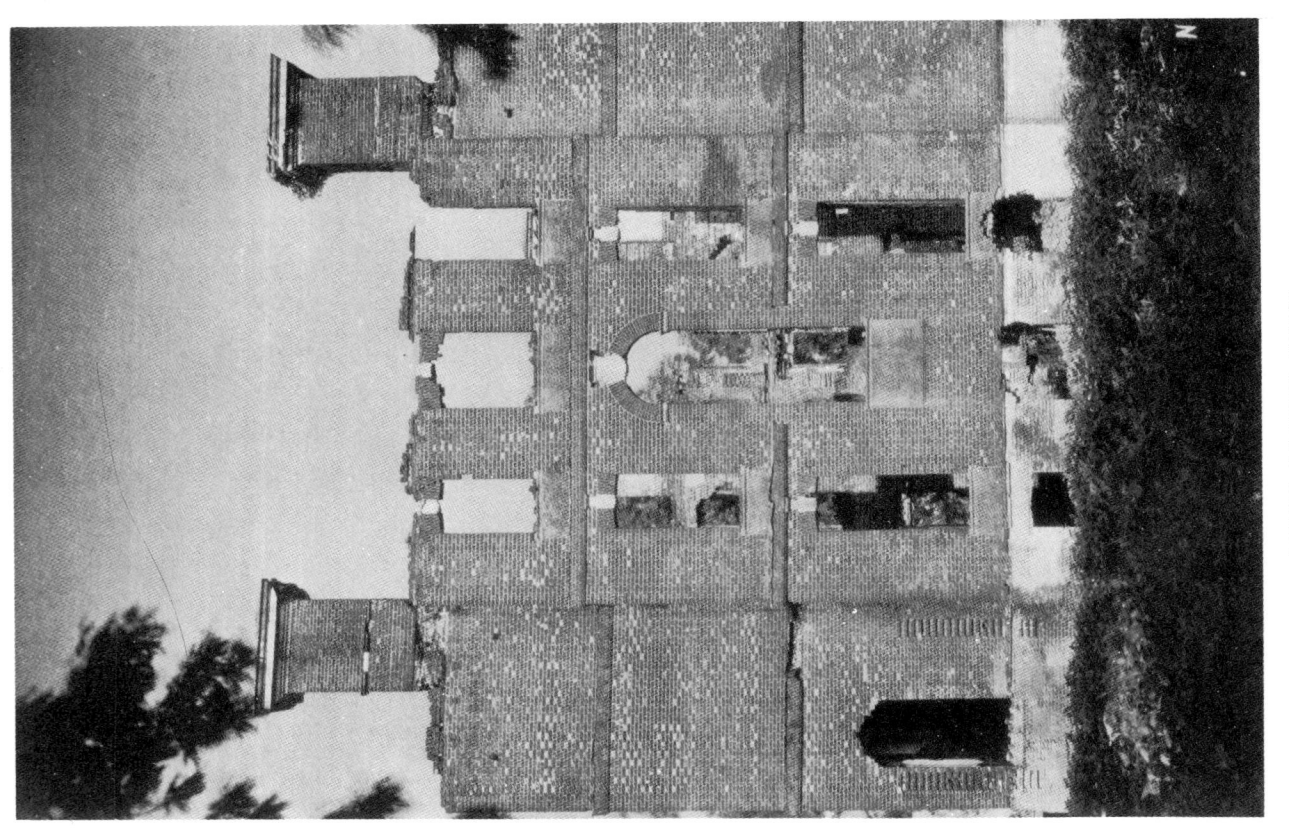
DETAIL OF WEST FRONT

WEST END OF SOUTH FRONT

Rosewell

RESTORED WEST ELEVATION
Scale, $\tfrac{3}{32}$ in. to the foot

Rosew

RESTORED NORTH ELEVA
Scale, $\frac{3}{32}$ in. to the foo

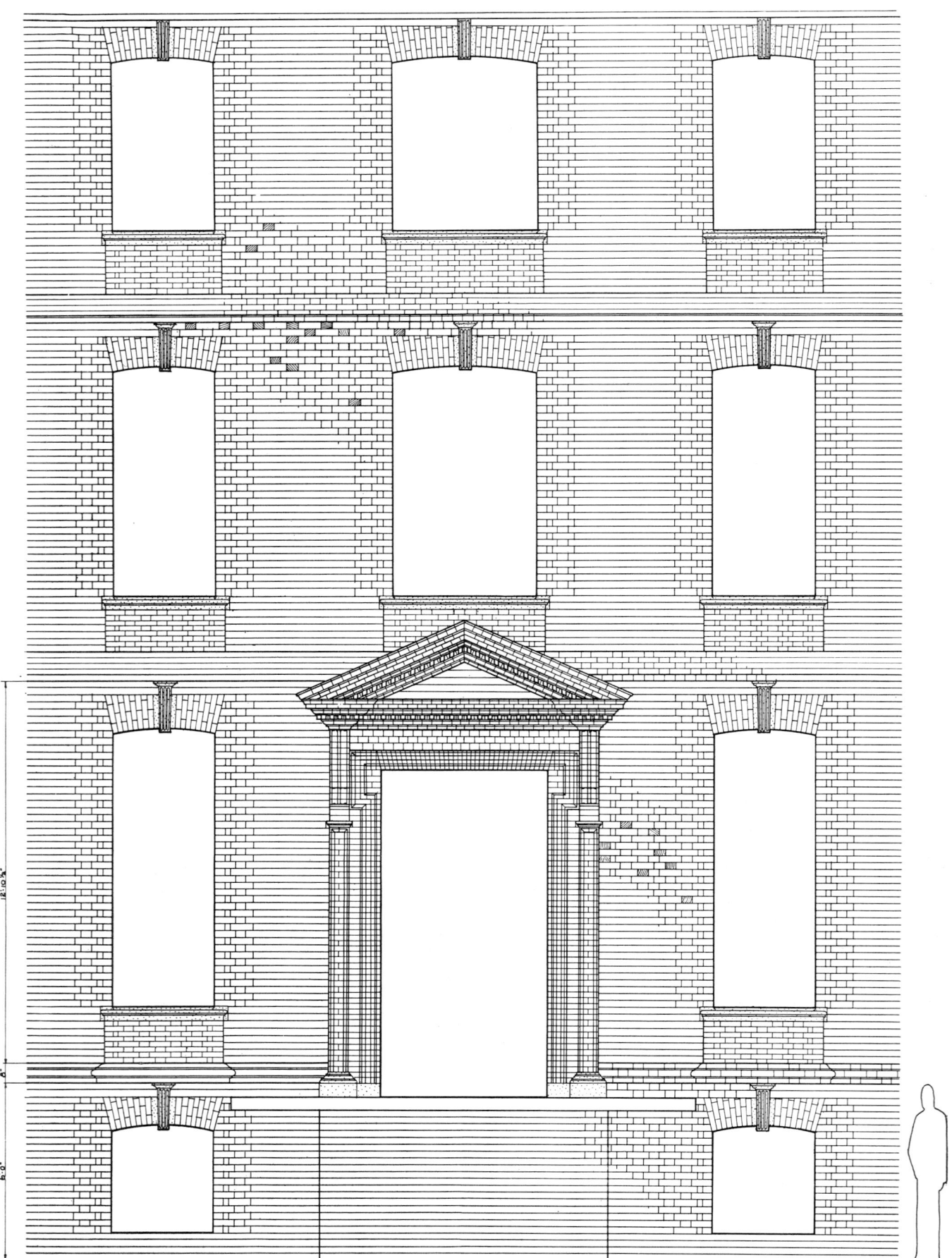

DETAIL OF NORTH ELEVATION

Carter's Grove

CARTER'S GROVE, JAMES CITY COUNTY
VIEW FROM THE SOUTH BEFORE ALTERATIONS

Carter's Grove

JAMES CITY COUNTY

1751

THE only remaining great house in the vicinity of Williamsburg, the Colonial capital of Virginia, is Carter Burwell's plantation house, Carter's Grove. It stands on the north bank of the James, about a half mile from the shore, and looks out from beneath a row of great shade trees, over high terraces and meadows, to the river in the distance. The mansion was built in 1751 by an English master mason, David Minitree, who came over to take charge of the work.

Carter Burwell, master of the estate, was the son of Nathaniel Burwell of Fairfield, and Elizabeth Carter, daughter of "King" Carter of Corotoman. No doubt the plantation was named in honor of his mother's famous family. Perhaps some of the vast wealth of "King" Carter may have been used in the building of the mansion. At any rate, it appears that Carter Burwell was proud of the name, and well he may have been, for the powerful Robert Carter, who because of his riches and influence had earned the sobriquet of "king," saw to it that his children married well. His son John married Elizabeth Hill of Shirley, and through this marriage Shirley came into the Carter family, in whose hands it has remained to the present day. One of his daughters, Judith, married Mann Page of Rosewell, and Anne married Benjamin Harrison of Berkeley, the neighboring estate to Westover. Robert built Nomini Hall on the Potomac; Charles Carter married Anne, daughter of William Byrd of Westover, and built Cleve on the Rappahannock. Sabine Hall, also on the Rappahannock, was built by Landon Carter, who married three times: first, an Armistead of Hesse, second, a Byrd of Westover, and last, a Wormeley of Rosegill. Mary married a Braxton and became mother of Carter Braxton. Lucy married into the Fitzhugh family. Thus in one generation did the Carters become "cousin" to nearly every one of importance in the colony.

A romance between Thomas Jefferson and Rebecca Burwell is connected with Carter's Grove. Jefferson, while a student at the College of William and Mary, was deeply in love with Miss Burwell, but that young lady preferred the attentions of young Jaquelin Ambler. Jefferson was held spellbound whenever he was in her presence, and was no doubt a rather awkward suitor. To his friend, John Page of Rosewell, he wrote in regard to his proposal: "If I am to meet with disappointment, the sooner I know it, the more of life I shall have to wear it off. . . . If Belinda (his fanciful name for her) will not accept of my service, it shall never be offered to another." Jefferson was only nineteen at the date of this writing and hence had many years to "wear it off," for his Belinda became

Domestic Colonial Architecture of Tidewater Virginia

the bride of the dashing young Ambler, and in time the mother of Mary Ambler, who later married John Marshall, Chief Justice of the United States.

Carter's Grove was occupied by the British during the Revolution, the estate was devastated and the house despoiled. The handrail of the splendid stairway still bears marks of the night of wild carousal when, if tradition is correct, Tarleton, wine-inflamed, rode his horse into the great hall, and, slashing all the way, rode up the stairs. Not long after the Revolution the estate passed out of the Burwell family.

Until 1928 the house practically retained its original appearance intact, certain minor changes having been made through the years. These notably were the addition of a broad porch across the south façade of the main house, and the replacement of the shingle roofs by slate on both the dependencies and the central building. The kitchen, formerly detached, was joined to the house by a low gambrel-roof connection. In 1928 the group of buildings was considerably altered. The modern porch happily was removed. The main roof was raised high enough to permit dormers to be placed in the former unbroken hip. The depth of the dependencies was increased and their original character greatly changed by the raising of the roofs, and by the new design of the dormers and chimney stacks. The former low connection between the kitchen and the main house was torn down. New closed arcades, with roofs approximately the height of the present dependencies, were built to join both kitchen and office buildings. The original semicircular stone steps at the north door of the main house were removed and placed before the doors of the dependencies.

While these changes are to be regretted from an architectural point of view, their necessity is admitted for the functioning of a great modern country house. The workmanship of both the interior and exterior alterations is irreproachable, and the treatment of the contemporary woodwork is magnificent.

The central building of Carter's Grove is rich in architectural detail, with two fine brick doorways, an elaborate water-table, and very rich dressings. The house stands well above the grade, and the strikingly bold mouldings of the water-table form a completely satisfactory base for the vast superstructure which rises above it. There are four full courses in the depth of this member: the top one being a cove, the second two forming an ovolo, which rests on one flush gauged course. At both north and south doorways this breaks out about the shafts of the brick door frames, and forms a base.

The walls of the main house are laid up of dark red brick in Flemish bond. Below the water-table the coursing is in English bond. There is no glazed brick in the central building. The corners of the house have elaborate rubbed dressings of alternating courses of stretcher and header, and header, closer and stretcher. The string course is returned short of the dressings to permit the latter to carry up to the bottom of the cornice without interruption. In itself the string is composed of four narrow gauged courses, laid in Flemish bond. The flat arches above all window openings are very elaborate, those of the first floor

Carter's Grove

CARTER'S GROVE BEFORE ALTERATIONS

being the most ornate. The jointing of the arch brick consists of two stretchers, alternating with header, closer, header, closer, and header. Those of the second-floor windows are somewhat simpler, being alternately header and stretcher, and the reverse. The color of the arches is carried down the jambs of the windows by superimposed rubbed headers and stretchers.

Perhaps the most interesting architectural features of the central building are the brick doorways of the north and south fronts. The former, though not so ornate, due to its being on the land side, is equally as satisfactory. It consists of a broad flat facing that projects beyond the wall of the house and rises to support a full moulded pediment. The brickwork is rubbed to a very fine joint and is skilfully laid. The south door differs from the north principally in that the flat piers become pilasters and are separated from the frame by a narrow brick face. The arch above the door is like that of the other entrance and in jointing is similar to the arches of the first-floor windows. The mouldings of the pediment are identical with those of the north door, with the exception that the horizontal member breaks around the pilaster.

The great chimney stacks are another noteworthy element of the design. The moulded brick caps, with those of the Nelson House, Yorktown, are undoubtedly the finest in Virginia. Rising high above the ridge, the shafts are first broken by a narrow necking. Above a frieze a cornice—apparently of the same mouldings as those of the doorways—corbels out and returns to the line of the stack by a rubbed brick wash. Two courses above the slope complete the caps.

Much of the exterior wood trim is old. The original heavy modillioned cornice carries around the eaves of the house. The window frames form broad architraves, and nearly all date from the erection of the build-

Domestic Colonial Architecture of Tidewater Virginia

ing. The sills on both first and second floors are moulded. There is no doubt that the sash is original. The muntins are very wide and much of the glass is old. The mouldings of the panels of the north door are exceedingly beautiful. The rails and stiles of the south door are old, but the panels themselves have been replaced.

The dependencies are laid up in Flemish bond with glazed headers both below and above the water-table. The corners of the buildings, the jambs and arches of both doors and windows, and the water-table itself, are of rubbed brick. The rake of the gables, as at the Thoroughgood House, are further accented by the use of glazed headers paralleling the verge board. Two vertical rows of glazed headers enrich both of the wide sides of the chimneys. Otherwise the glazing is omitted from the stacks, the line of departure in the bonding being at the intersection of the verge board with the ridge. The dependency to the west of the great house had two gabled dormers across the north façade and three across the south. The building to the east of the mansion, the original kitchen, had three gabled dormers across both north and south fronts.

In the restoration presented herewith, only the doors of these detached structures are conjectural. The former modern addition to the east of the house was eliminated in the drawing. The degree of scale obtained by the wide window spacing in the central building is worthy of note. The great wall surfaces and the low, unbroken slope of the roof created an atmosphere of spaciousness found in no other great house standing to-day in Virginia.

The interior contains the finest Georgian woodwork in the State.

NORTH DOOR

DEPENDENCY BEFORE ALTERATIONS

SOUTH DOOR

Carter's Grove

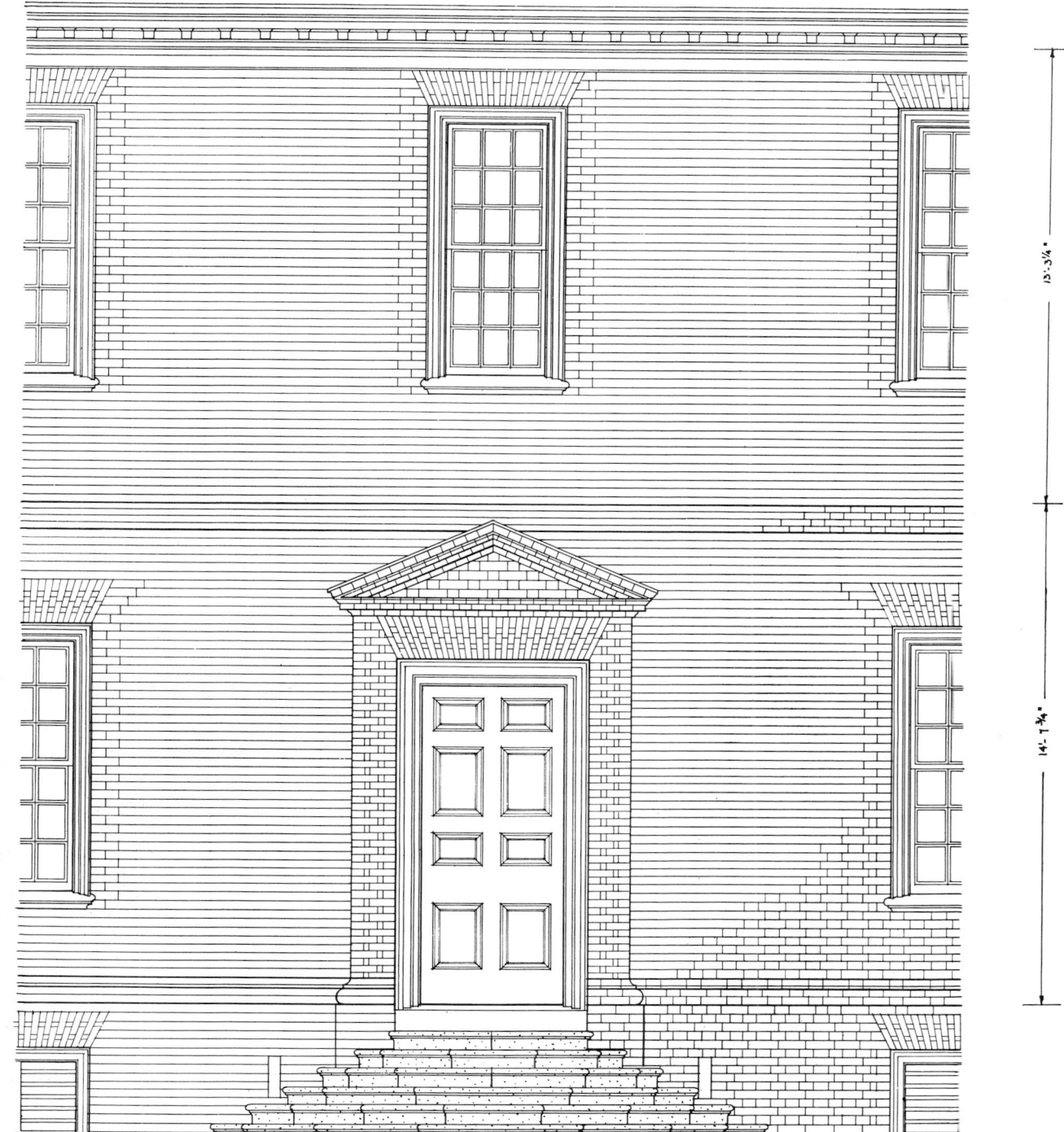

DETAIL OF NORTH ELEVATION BEFORE ALTERATIONS
Scale, ¼ in. to the foot

Carter's G

NORTH ELEVATION BEFORE ALTE
(EASTERN CONNECTION OMIT
Scale, $\tfrac{3}{32}$ in. to the foot

Domestic Colonial Architecture of Tidewater Virginia

WEST ELEVATION BEFORE ALTERATION
STEPS SUBSTITUTED FOR SOUTH PORCH
Scale, $\frac{3}{32}$ in. to the foot

Carter's Grove

NORTH FRONT BEFORE ALTERATIONS

SOUTH FRONT IN 1931

Cleve

CLEVE, KING GEORGE COUNTY

Cleve

KING GEORGE COUNTY

1754

On the north bank of the Rappahannock River near Dogue Post Office stand the scarred remains of Cleve, one of the least known and most interesting of mid-eighteenth-century houses in Virginia. The interior and roof of the building were destroyed by fire early in the nineteenth century, at which time the house was rebuilt and altered. Again in 1917 it was burned, and what remained of the walls above the first-floor level was pulled down.

Charles Carter, son of Robert, "King" Carter of Corotoman, built Cleve in 1754, and its magnificence vied with the seats of his brothers, John of Shirley, Robert of Nomini, Landon of Sabine Hall, and with the homes of his sisters, Anne of Berkeley and Judith of Rosewell. Westover, whence came Anne Byrd, his second wife, did not surpass Cleve, and Carter's Grove, plantation house of his nephew, Carter Burwell, was no finer.

Cleve differs from the other brick dwellings of Virginia in surpassing them all in richness of stone dressings. Ornamental stonework was used first at Rosewell (1720–30), Gloucester County, in the windowsills, keystones in the window arches, and in parapet and chimney caps. At the Nelson House (1740), Yorktown, stone keys are again employed and quoins are first used at the corners. Gunston Hall (1758), Fairfax County, and the Tebbs house, Dumfries, approach Cleve in richness, but in both the quoining is restricted to the corners of the building and the window arches of the latter only are keyed with stone. At Cleve stone is found in all of the architectural features: the water-table, window arches, sills and jambs, doorway and quoining of the corners.

The dependencies which once flanked the main house have long since disappeared, perhaps in the fire that gutted the mansion in 1800. As rebuilt, the interior of the main house was according to the taste of the period. Panelling above the dado gave way to plaster. The elaborate Georgian stair, probably reminiscent of that at Carter's Grove, was replaced by a delicate Adamesque design, and the heavy modillioned cornices were replaced by others enriched by pierced dentils, reeded ornament and auger-holes in patterns. The overmantels alone retained panelling above the dado. This woodwork, inadequate as it was in replacing earlier work, had unusual interest as illustrating a period in which there was little building activity in the Tidewater, outside of Norfolk.

Cleve was celebrated for its fine collection of Georgian portraits. Rows of Carters looked down on the many generations that passed

Domestic Colonial Architecture of Tidewater Virginia

through the great hall. Charles Carter was extremely fond of dancing, and directed in his will that his sons and daughters be made proficient in the art. The last of the original name to own Cleve was St. Leger Landon Carter, from whom it passed to the Lewises, descendants of Fielding Lewis of Kenmore and his wife Betty, sister of George Washington.

The portion of the house remaining, other than an unarchitectural extension to the west, is the complete basement to the top of the water-table, and the southwest corner of the building which now forms a pier for a modern water tank. Two-thirds of the area of the former mansion is covered by a modern frame structure, and under this remain many of the original brick partitions shown on the accompanying plan.

The basement walls are of brick, laid in English bond, with gauged flat arches over the window openings. The water-table is of moulded stone; above it the corner quoins are rusticated, below they are flush with the face of the wall. A strip of brickwork, laid in Flemish bond, remains flanking the quoins, giving the relation of the brick and stone coursing. This makes the restoration presented herewith accurate in vertical dimensions; the horizontals being determined by the existing basement walls and window openings.

The stone trim, removed when the walls were demolished, is piled in long rows near the entrance to the grounds. These fragments were examined and measured, and their locations in the measured detail were determined by photographs taken before the fire.

Both the jambs of the first-floor and second-floor windows were trimmed with flush stone quoins, and the voussoirs of the flat arches were stepped up to receive keystones, which on the lower windows were surmounted by moulded caps; moulded stone sills extended across the entire width of the window opening and the stone trim. The architecture of the doorway was similar to that of the windows, but here both quoins and arch stones were lightly rusticated. Fragments of the entrance steps were found nearby; their exact arrangement on the detail is conjectural, but the general design is taken from a photograph. No sinkages were found for iron work. The height of the platform above the grade would, however, indicate that rails were used.

In the accompanying restoration of the building the gables shown in the photograph were considered as a part of the alterations subsequent to the first fire. Their inferior brickwork would indicate that a hipped roof originally covered the house; a conclusion borne out by the almost universal popularity of this type of roof. The spacing of the windows was determined by the location of those existing in the basement wall. Their height was obtained by the stone coursing shown in the photograph.

Cleve and Carter's Grove were built almost simultaneously by related families. In all probability David Minitree, the master mason of the latter, was employed on Cleve. This might explain the remarkable similarity in the planning and fenestration of the two buildings. The north door at Cleve was flanked on either side by two windows, as at

Cleve

Carter's Grove, which lighted rooms to the east and west of the stair hall. The south elevations were also similar. On the right and left of the central door were three windows. Those immediately to either side lighted a salon which, from evidence still remaining, was separated from the stair hall proper by an arched opening.

The situation, some of the original landscape work, and contemporary outbuildings, give additional interest to the remains of Cleve.

NORTH FRONT AFTER THE FIRE

Domestic Colonial Architecture of Tidewater Virginia

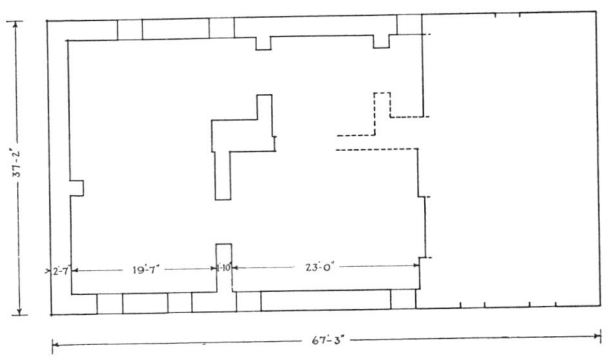

PLAN OF EXISTING FOUNDATIONS AT CLEVE

Scale, $\frac{3}{64}$ in. to the foot

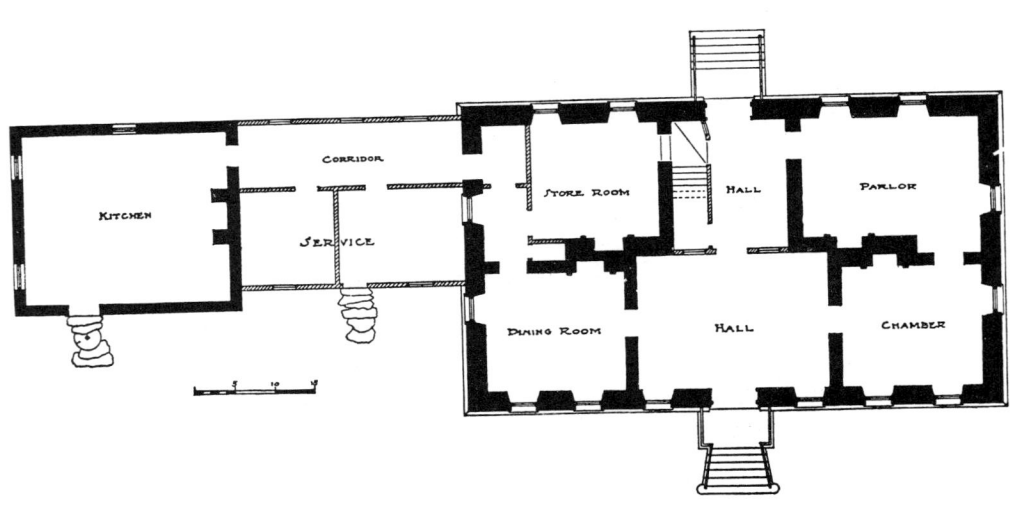

PLAN BEFORE THE FIRE, BY FRANK C. BALDWIN

Scale, $\frac{3}{64}$ in. to the foot

Cleve

CONJECTURAL RESTORED SOUTH ELEVATION
Scale, $\frac{3}{32}$ in. to the foot

Domestic Colonial Architecture of Tidewater Virginia

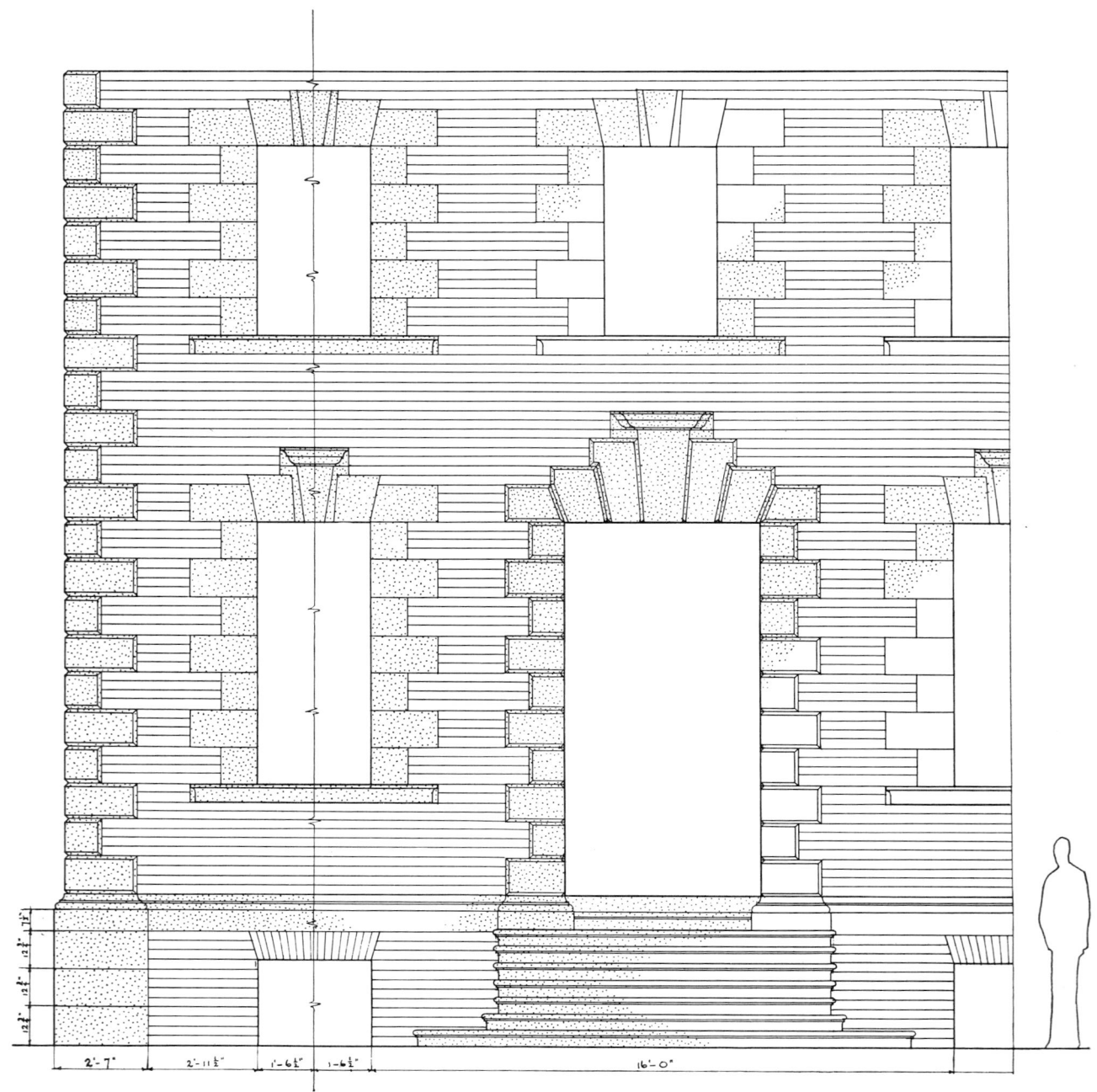

CONJECTURAL DETAIL, SOUTH FRONT OF CLEVE

Scale, ¼ in. to the foot

Wilton

WILTON, HENRICO COUNTY

Wilton

HENRICO COUNTY

1754

ON the north bank of the James, six miles below Richmond, William Randolph III built Wilton in 1754. The first Randolph in Virginia came to the colony in 1660 and settled at Turkey Island, nearby. The latter house stood until the War between the States, when it was shelled by Federal gunboats and destroyed. William Randolph I became a man of wealth and influence, was a member of the Council and a member of the House of Burgesses.

Turkey Island is not far below the site of Dutch Gap, where, during the administration of Sir Thomas Dale, a city was laid out which, it was hoped, would become the new capital of Virginia. It was to be called Henrico or Henricopolis, after the son of King James. Here in 1619 the first university in America was proposed to be built, the land set aside and money amounting to $100,000 subscribed. But the infant institution was not to be; on Good Friday morning, 1622, the great Indian Massacre put an end to the project. Governor Berkeley, who came to Virginia in 1642, just after the colony was recovering from the effects of the slaughter, was in power until his recall in 1677, and thanked God that there were no free schools in Virginia. Thus it was that until 1693 no institution of higher learning was chartered.

The Randolphs were a large family and settled in many parts of the colony. So numerous did they become that they took the names of their places to distinguish one from another. Thus we have John Randolph of Roanoke, William Randolph of Wilton, the Randolphs of Tuckahoe, of Chatsworth, of Varina, of Curles, of Bremo and of Dungeness.

William Randolph, the builder of Wilton, had a beautiful daughter, Anne, of whom Thomas Jefferson was greatly enamored. Benjamin Harrison of Brandon, his chum while at the College of William and Mary, was also an ardent admirer of this lady, and offered the same interference that Jaquelin Ambler had shown when Jefferson went courting at Carter's Grove; and again was Jefferson the loser, for "Nancy Wilton," as Anne was called, became the bride of young Harrison.

Wilton was the home of Mary Randolph, who married Archibald Cary of Ampthill, across the river, and of Innes Randolph, the poet. Lafayette, Lord Conwallis, and George Washington were entertained at the famous house at various times.

Peyton Randolph, son of the builder, was the second owner. His daughters inherited the house and, just before the War between the States, sold it to Colonel William Carter Knight.

Domestic Colonial Architecture of Tidewater Virginia

Wilton was damaged during the Revolution and the War between the States. Just before the latter war, breastworks were thrown up along the river's edge, which still may be seen. The house as it stands to-day, robbed of its dependent buildings, suffers in the degree of grandeur possessed by other James River estates. Its interest lies almost wholly in its mass and detail. The elaborate wood doorways of both fronts of the house are unique of their type in Tidewater Virginia, the President's House (1732), Williamsburg, having the only other door feature not of brick or stone.

Wilton is well cared for and, though not occupied, is open to visitors. Its interior is richly panelled on both floors, there being no plaster in the house except the ceilings.

The south front looks over a sloping lawn to the James River in the distance. Opposite, but further to the west, stood Ampthill, the neighboring estate, now supplanted by the towering stacks of the duPont rayon plant recently built on the property.

The north elevation has been materially disfigured by a modern porch that covers the location of the pediment over the door and shades the innermost windows which flank it. As in the south elevation, there are five windows across the second floor of this front. Here the sills are moulded and the sash is original, the latter consisting of small panes of glass, divided by heavy muntins. The south front suffers by the introduction of single-light sash into the windows of both first-floor and second-floor openings. The windows on the first floor of this front have been lengthened nearly to the floor line.

The mass of the house, seen in perspective, is far more satisfactory than the drawing would indicate. The moderately low hip roof springs from a rather delicately detailed cornice, composed of both dentils and modillions. Two tall chimneys rise at each outer end of the house and the window grouping on either side of these makes this elevation unusual. The openings are tall and narrow, and light closets formed out of the space on either side of the stacks which, as at Westover (1726), Charles City County, are built within the wall line of the house.

The central doorway of the south front is complete with the exception of the bases. It consists of fluted pilasters with crudely carved Ionic caps, surmounted by an architrave, a pulvinated frieze and a modillioned pediment. It is reasonable to believe that the portion of the north doorway destroyed by the introduction of the porch is similar to that of the south, the caps and pilasters being identical. A modern brick and concrete floor covers all evidence of the former stair treatment. The eight-panelled door itself is a single valve and its mouldings are exceedingly rich. A transom of eight lights is over the south door, while the north door, being taller, is surmounted by a transom of only four lights.

The richness of the dressings at Wilton is appreciable at a great distance. The brick of the main walls is of a cool, lavender red, while the rubbed brick is an extremely bright vermilion. Both corners and window openings are rubbed the depth of a header, closer, and stretcher on one course, and by a stretcher and header on the next. The arches are elaborately jointed on both first and second floors.

Wilton

Those of the first floor consist of header, closer, and stretcher, and the reverse, and those of the second floor of alternating header and stretcher, and the reverse.

The brick below the water-table is laid up in English bond. The arches over the basement windows are actually all of stretchers, but this fact is disguised by incising a line across alternating bricks and filling the incision with mortar, simulating a joint. This practice occurs frequently in the bonding of moulded brickwork about doorways. The water-table, of gauged brick, consists of a cove and torus. Above it the bonding becomes Flemish. The string course at the line of the second floor is rubbed and is also laid in Flemish bond.

In recent years, the roof of the house has been covered with slate. A nondescript frame addition practically covers the east end of the building. A few fine trees shade the lawn, and scattered about are several old outbuildings. There are no visible remains of the dependencies which once flanked the house.

The restoration drawing is of the north façade. The pediment of the doorway is that of the south elevation and the stairway alone is conjectural. In the detail the pediment over the doorway was measured and drawn from the existing south door. The original treatment of the steps is concealed by modern work and therefore was omitted from the detail.

DETAIL OF SOUTH DOORWAY

Domestic Colonial Architecture of Tidewater Virginia

WEST SIDE

WILTON FROM THE NORTHWEST

RESTORED NORTH ELEVATION

RESTORED WEST ELEVATION
Scale, $\frac{3}{32}$ in. to the foot

Domestic Colonial Architecture of Tidewater Virginia

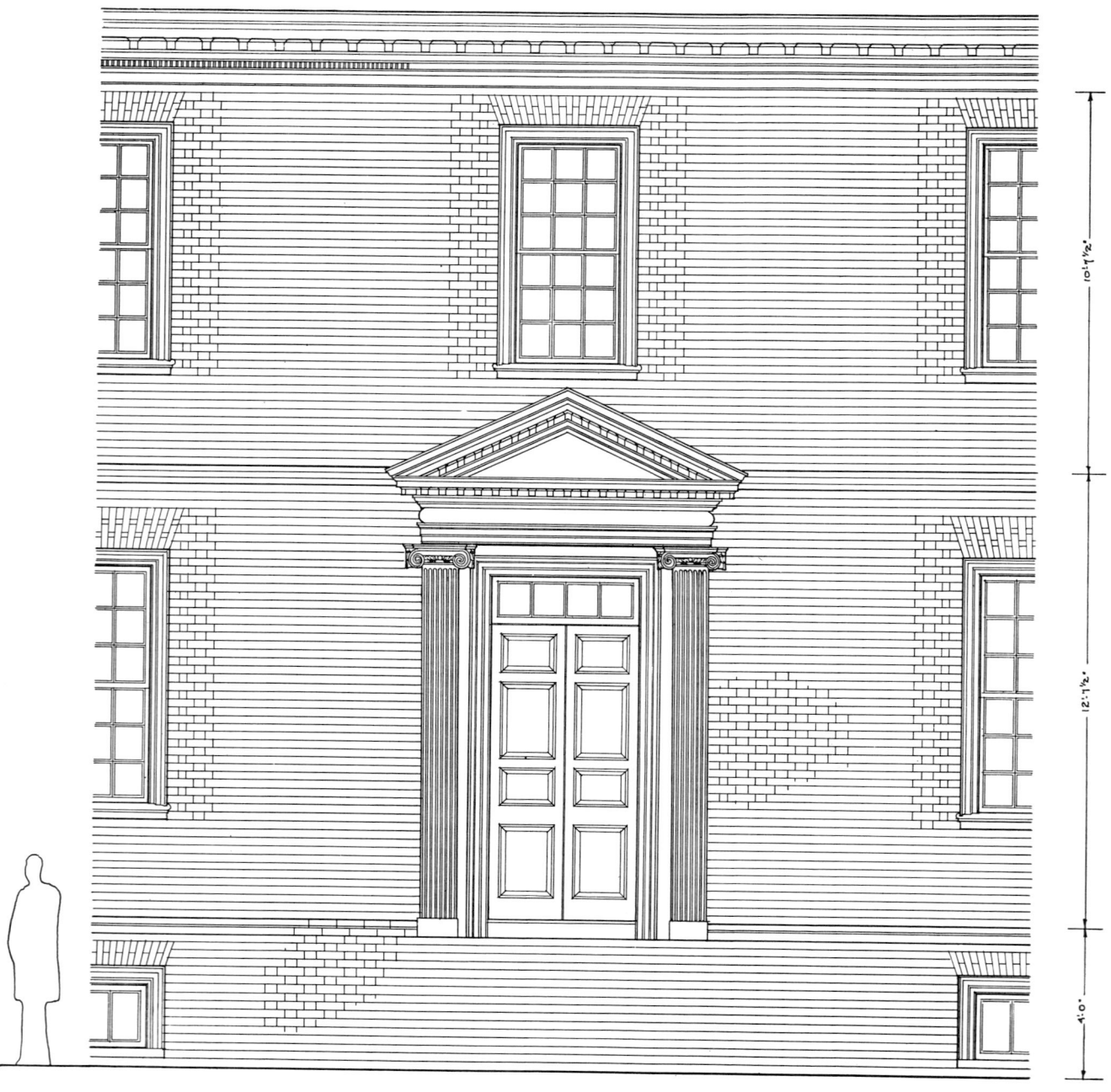

DETAIL OF NORTH ELEVATION
Scale, ¼ in. to the foot

Mount Airy

MOUNT AIRY, RICHMOND COUNTY

Mount Airy

RICHMOND COUNTY

1758

Mount Airy, the most academic of Virginia mansions, was built by Colonel John Tayloe in 1758, upon land acquired by his grandfather in the middle of the previous century. The Tayloes, one of the wealthiest families in the colonies, were allied with almost all of the great names of the Rappahannock region. They kept a famous string of racehorses and maintained a private racetrack at Mount Airy. On the marriage of his daughter Rebecca to Francis Lightfoot Lee in 1769, Colonel John Tayloe built Menokin for her as a wedding gift, and the kinship of the two houses is apparent in both architecture and material, each being largely of local stone. When Washington became the capital of the United States, Benjamin Ogle Tayloe built as a town house The Octagon, designed by Thornton, now headquarters of the American Institute of Architects. While The Octagon and Menokin have long since passed from the family, Mount Airy has always remained in the possession of the male line and is now the residence of William H. Tayloe, of Richmond, and the Misses Tayloe. The house has much the effect of a manor house of the Georgian period in the Cotswold district. Classic forms here reach their most scholarly use in pre-Revolutionary Virginia, and this classicism is accentuated by the fact that the composition is entirely in stone. The house lacks the formality of approach that is so customary in the James River estates, but the picturesqueness of the park, once filled with deer, is very reminiscent of England. This informality is in contrast to the extreme symmetry of the plan of the house itself and of the contiguous grounds.

The rise on which Mount Airy stands was graded to form a base for it. Immediately beyond the building and following its perimeter, the grade lowers by means of a short terrace. The grounds widen out beyond: to the north in a circular entrance drive, to the east in a lawn, to the west in a formal boxwood garden, and to the south in a vast parterre. From the parterre the river is visible several miles away across the bottom lands that lie at the foot of the lateral ridge on which the house is built. The familiar long walk of English gardens, bordered by magnificent box, terminates the pleasaunce to the west, and flanking it on the axis of the house are the ruins of the orangery. This is a contemporary brick structure of which only a part of the front wall exists, but the design can still be discerned: an arcade of tall windows flanked by pylons which are pierced by arched doorways.

The semicircular forecourt in front of the house is defined by the terrace, which also carries in front of the immediate dependencies. The court is reached by a short flight of moulded stone steps, on the main axis, flanked by elaborately carved stone urns on pedestals. These rest on a low retaining wall which is further decorated by squat acorn finials. The only planting in the court is a pair of fine old hollies.

In a fire which gutted the interior of the house in 1840, the roof and all exterior wood trim and glazing were destroyed. The effectiveness of the design is much diminished by the loss of the Georgian cornice and pediments and especially of the roof. The elaboration of the stone architecture is interesting in the extreme, and is unique.

The north entrance to the house is within a loggia of three openings divided by pilastered piers, which support a full stone entablature. The side walls of the loggia are treated with niches faced with architraves and covered with pediments supported on consoles. Unfortunately the inside wall sheds no light on the form of the original doorway. Above the portico a continuous pedestal provides a base for three windows with fully moulded architraves which are eared at the top and swing out in pseudo-consoles at the bottom. The loggia is contained within a pavilion which rests on the moulded water-table that carries around the whole building. The composition is rather too cramped to be entirely successful. The quoins of this pavilion, as well as its undecorated wall surface, are rusticated with a square sinkage, not V-sunk as is the rest of the quoining in the building. The south pavilion is similar to the north in general disposition of elements, but a triple arcade contains the entrance here and no moulded trim is used, the whole being in V-sunk rustication. On both main elevations the pavilions are flanked by two windows on each floor, which are framed by moulded architraves. The corners of the building are quoined, and a string course carries through at the line of the second floor.

The pavilions and all of the trimming stone is buff, probably a mixture of English Portland and native Aquia Creek stone. The ashlar is a local gold brown stone laid in random courses. This contrast of the light and dark emphasizes the architectural features of the house.

Both end elevations are treated architecturally with pavilions. The east end is the more elaborate but has suffered more from alterations. The present arched opening was formerly a window lighting the stair hall. This and the narrow flanking windows form a variant of the Palladian motive, which was later to become so hackneyed. They are knit together in the composition by projecting quoin blocks that are laid up with the architraves in the mullions. These blocks also occur in the arch of the central window and in the outside jambs of the flanking windows where they abut the quoin strips that form the pavilions. All three windows have heavy keystones which, with the impost blocks, have extra projection, giving the design good relief. Above a string course the second-floor windows have the same grouping as those below. Their trim, however, is a simple stone surround, and the central arch is a low ellipse. A slight asymmetry in the placement of the windows in the pavilion may be noticed.

Mount Airy

THE NORTH FRONT

The west end is much less elaborate but is equally satisfactory. The same rusticated quoin strips occur, as well as the string course. A secondary belt, which is used on the walls at the side of the pavilion on the east end, here traverses the entire end at the head of the windows. The axial feature is a window beneath a pediment that is supported on Doric piers. Above is a single window with moulded trim, and single windows with unmoulded stone surrounds occur in each floor to the side of the pavilion on this, as well as the opposite end. The field of both pavilions is of local stone.

The covered passageways connecting the house and the dependencies are each a quadrant in plan, together forming the semicircular forecourt. They are built entirely of local stone. The court elevations have a narrow central door with a single window on either side. The garden sides are perhaps somewhat altered and are covered with vines, making it difficult to determine the original design. At present several openings divided by wood posts occur near the junction with the central building. There are other unimportant openings to the side. The connections are covered with shed roofs that slope away from the forecourt. The roofs are raised near the house to allow headroom for the stair that ascends to the level of the main floor. The consequent break in the court wall is treated with wood brackets, perhaps original, decorated with primitive scroll carving.

The dependencies themselves are virtually square and are two stories high. They are built entirely of local stone, carefully coursed. The quoins and string course are rusticated, but the windows lack any stone trim. All of the ashlar is scored as if it were intended for plastering. The front elevations have two windows on each floor, the court three and the side four. The latter are the most interesting façades, as the fenestration seems the most satisfactory. A stone doorway replaces one of the lower windows on each of these elevations. The handling of the quoining in them is ingenious. The short quoins are raised

Domestic Colonial Architecture of Tidewater Virginia

half an inch above the plane of the wall while the long ones and the lintel and keystone are raised an inch and a quarter. Rustication as a means of emphasizing the joints is accordingly unnecessary. These openings have the original sheathed doors which are both unusual and effective. The glazing and cornice are of the same period as the trim of the main house, although the fire stopped short at the connections. The original hip-on-hip roofs of the dependencies remain, with the chimneys projecting through the centre. On these chimneys the caps are of the buff trimming stone; a full cornice above a pseudo-architrave, a strip of local stone separating them.

The small-scale elevation presented here shows only the woodwork and roof restored. Of the latter, the form is clearly indicated by the existing roof at Blandfield, with the same chimney grouping, and that at Menokin. The chimney caps are similar to those on the dependencies, and the pineapple is said to have occurred at the apex of the roof, as at Shirley, Charles City County, and Brandon, Prince George County. The glazing is conjectural, but according to Colonial glass sizes. In the connections, the design of the doors also is conjectural.

Mount Airy presents an exterior, with its entourage, exemplifying in an unusual completeness the finest type of eighteenth-century Virginia mansion. The loss of the original exterior wood trim is unfortunate but is unnoticeable from a short distance. In richness of stone detail no house in Virginia surpassed it and Palladianism hardly reached a more elaborate expression in the colonies than here. The outbuildings remain much in their entirety and are particularly interesting. Fortunately, the dependencies still possess their original interior trim. The magnificence of the woodwork of the main house may only be surmised from the fragments of cornice that were rescued from the fire, now made into mantels. These are bed-moulds, of three members, all richly carved in high relief.

It is with surprise that one notices that the original interior trim is gone. The house is so full of superb furniture, portraits, silver, china, and memorabilia of the eighteenth century that the Victorian woodwork hardly intrudes itself.

W. H. T. Squires

THE RIVER FRONT

Mount Airy

DETAIL OF NORTH ELEVATION
Scale, ¼ in. to the foot

Mount A

RESTORED NORTH ELE
Scale, $\tfrac{3}{32}$ in. to the

Domestic Colonial Architecture of Tidewater Virginia

DETAIL OF EAST ELEVATION
Scale, ¼ in. to the foot

Mount Airy

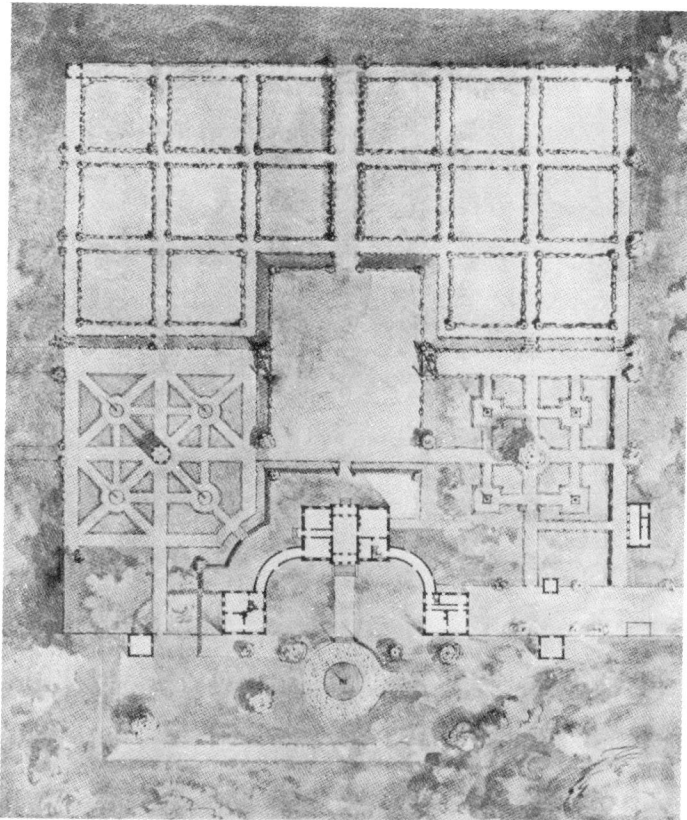

Courtesy of F. C. Baldwin, Esq.
RESTORED PLOT PLAN

DETAIL OF ENTRANCE PIERS

DETAIL OF THE EAST ELEVATION

EAST SIDE, SHOWING DEPENDENCY

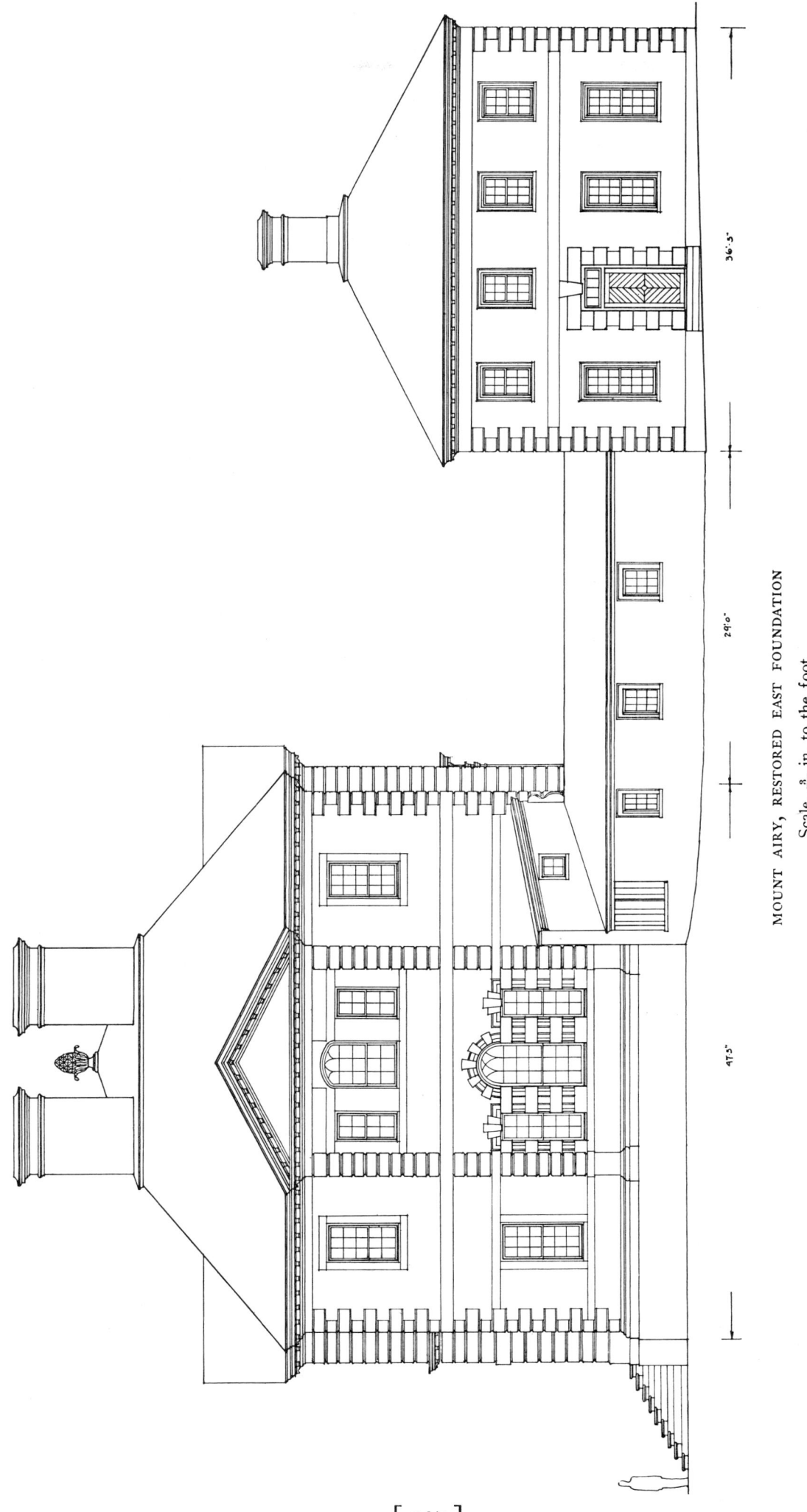

MOUNT AIRY, RESTORED EAST FOUNDATION
Scale, 3/32 in. to the foot

Blandfield

BLANDFIELD, ESSEX COUNTY

Blandfield

ESSEX COUNTY

1760-1770

On the south side of the Rappahannock, not more than eight miles above the colonial town of Tappahannock, an inconspicuous dirt road swings off the Tidewater Trail toward the river. Following this through woods and fields for several miles, the old home of the Beverleys is at last reached, almost hidden by great trees. The completeness of Blandfield is remarkable. It is surprising that a house of such grandeur should have so long remained practically unknown to architects. There seems no explanation other than the remoteness of the location.

Robert Beverley, the first to come to Virginia, arrived in the colony in 1663. In 1670 he was made Clerk of the House of Burgesses, and during Bacon's Rebellion served as a Major in the King's Army. He died in 1687 and left over fifty thousand acres to his children, the most prominent being Robert Beverley, the first native historian of the colony. His "History of Virginia" was published in 1705 and a second edition followed in 1722. This was the Beverley who was with Alexander Spotswood, Lieutenant-Governor of Virginia, when the latter, with his Knights of the Golden Horseshoe, rode out into the unknown West and were the first to see the noble Blue Ridge Mountains.

There is no record or evidence of the type of house that served through the one hundred years before Blandfield was built. Colonel William Beverley, son of the historian, married Elizabeth Bland and built the present house about 1760, naming it in honor of her family, the Blands of the James. His mother was Ursula Byrd, daughter of William Byrd I of Westover.

During the War between the States Blandfield was despoiled. The barns were raided and cattle and horses were seized for army purposes, and it is said that Federal soldiers removed much of the fine furniture which the old house contained. Even the family portraits were not spared, but were carted down to the plantation wharf to a gunboat which carried away the treasures of six generations of Beverleys. The fine pieces that remain in the house bear witness to the glory that was once Blandfield's. The house still remains in the family, one of the few Virginia places in the hands of a direct descendant of the builder.

The house, all of brick, is of a three-part composition, comprising a dominating central building connected to lower two-story dependencies by one-story shed-roof passages.

The design of the main house in its elements is reminiscent of Mount Airy, across the river. The roof is a hip-on-hip, unbroken except for the pediments of the pavilions. Four tall central chimneys pierce the second slope. Their caps are well designed, though simple, being of projecting courses brought back to the line of the shaft by a cement wash.

Both fronts of the house are substantially identical. Each consists of a central pavilion which is flanked on either side by two windows on each floor. Across the upper part of the pavilions are three windows, the central one of which was cut down into a door to give access to a neo-Classic porch, added when the house was altered in 1854. The pavilions being wider than those at Mount Airy, the fenestration seems less cramped and the effect is more satisfactory.

A string course carries around the house at the line of the second floor. The windows on the first floor are the same width and spacing as those above, but are considerably taller, due to the greater ceiling height of the lower rooms. The moulded water-table, a cove and an ovolo, forms the offset at the base of the building.

The flat arches over the openings of the main house are probably the most conspicuous feature of the design. Their splay is tremendous, being nearly forty-five degrees. The effect, however, is not as awkward as the drawing would indicate. The dressing around the windows at Blandfield is as rich as any house in Virginia and reaches out to the full splay of the arches themselves. In the main house, the brick, laid up in Flemish bond, is exceedingly large, four courses measuring 13½ inches. The rubbed brick, still exhibiting its original bright vermilion, is very effective against the duller tones of the walls.

The brickwork of the passages and dependencies is not of the same size and richness as that of the house. It lays up four courses to 12½ inches. The difference in scale between the principal and lesser buildings, derived from the difference in the size of the brick, is noteworthy. Like the main house, the brickwork in both dependencies and passages is Flemish bond.

A great deal of the charm of Blandfield lies in the placing of the dependencies, which enclose a rose garden in the forecourt. The front wall of the passages practically lines with the face of the house, which is on the same plane as the rear walls of the dependencies. Thus communication with these outbuildings is obtained through their rear walls. This scheme of connection at Blandfield is unique. Seen from the garden it is most picturesque, but it suffers on the side elevation.

With the exception of the cornices of the main house, passages and dependencies, the exterior woodwork dates from 1854. In that year the central building was entirely remodelled by Colonel William Beverley, then the owner. Everything Georgian was removed; and plain plaster walls were substituted for the panelling, and mediocre wood trim was used around the doors and windows. Nothing old remains within the house but the floors. The woodwork in the dependencies escaped, however, and, although simple, is of considerable interest.

The scale detail presented herewith shows the windows glazed as at present, but since it does not pertain to the subject, the neo-Classic porch was omitted in order to show the entrance motive complete. In the restoration only the sash throughout the building, the front steps of the main house and the doors

Blandfield

of the passages, are conjectural. There is no evidence that there was an iron rail on the steps, but its use seems likely, due to the proximity of the basement windows to the platform, prohibiting the employment of any other type of stairs. Georgian stone steps with moulded nosings have been built into the porch of the river front of the house. These are undoubtedly the original entrance steps.

Like Mount Airy, Blandfield is situated on one of the low ridges that rise beyond the bottom lands of the Rappahannock. Its site is unusually fine and from the river side the house is very impressive, standing at the top of a long slope, even though its receding wings are concealed by the brow of the ridge. The garden front with its projecting dependencies gives a more accurate impression of the real size of the mansion, but is impossible to photograph in its entirety because of the dense foliage which surrounds the buildings.

Mr. Samuel Athawes   April 15, 1771

I have been some Time employed in building an House, & as I am desirous of fitting it up in a plain neat Manner, I w^d willingly consult the present Fashion, for you know that foolish Passion had made its way, Even into this remote Region. I observed that Ld B. had hung a room with plain blue Paper & border'd it with a narrow stripe of gilt Leather, wch I thought had a pretty effect. I shall also want some Chimney Pieces of the Grey Marble, perfectly plain, upon the Model of several I have seen imported here late Years, viz. after the common Method at the Sides, with a Piece of the same Kind of Marble at the Top, to project or rather to extend something farther than the Supporters—My Chimneys, are 4 Feet wide— I am told they are cheap, & I think them infinitely neater than the Embassed or figured ones. I must beg therefore you will Enquire into the Price both of the Paper & Chimney Pieces & inform me by the Autumn of 1772.—(From a letter to Mr. Samuel Athawes, of London, in the letterbook of Robert Beverley for the years 1761–93, now in the Library of Congress.)

NORTH FRONT

Bland

RESTORED SOUTH ELE
Scale, $\frac{3}{32}$ in. to the

BLANDFIELD, SOUTH FRONT

Blandfield

DETAIL OF SOUTH ELEVATION
Scale, ¼ in. to the foot

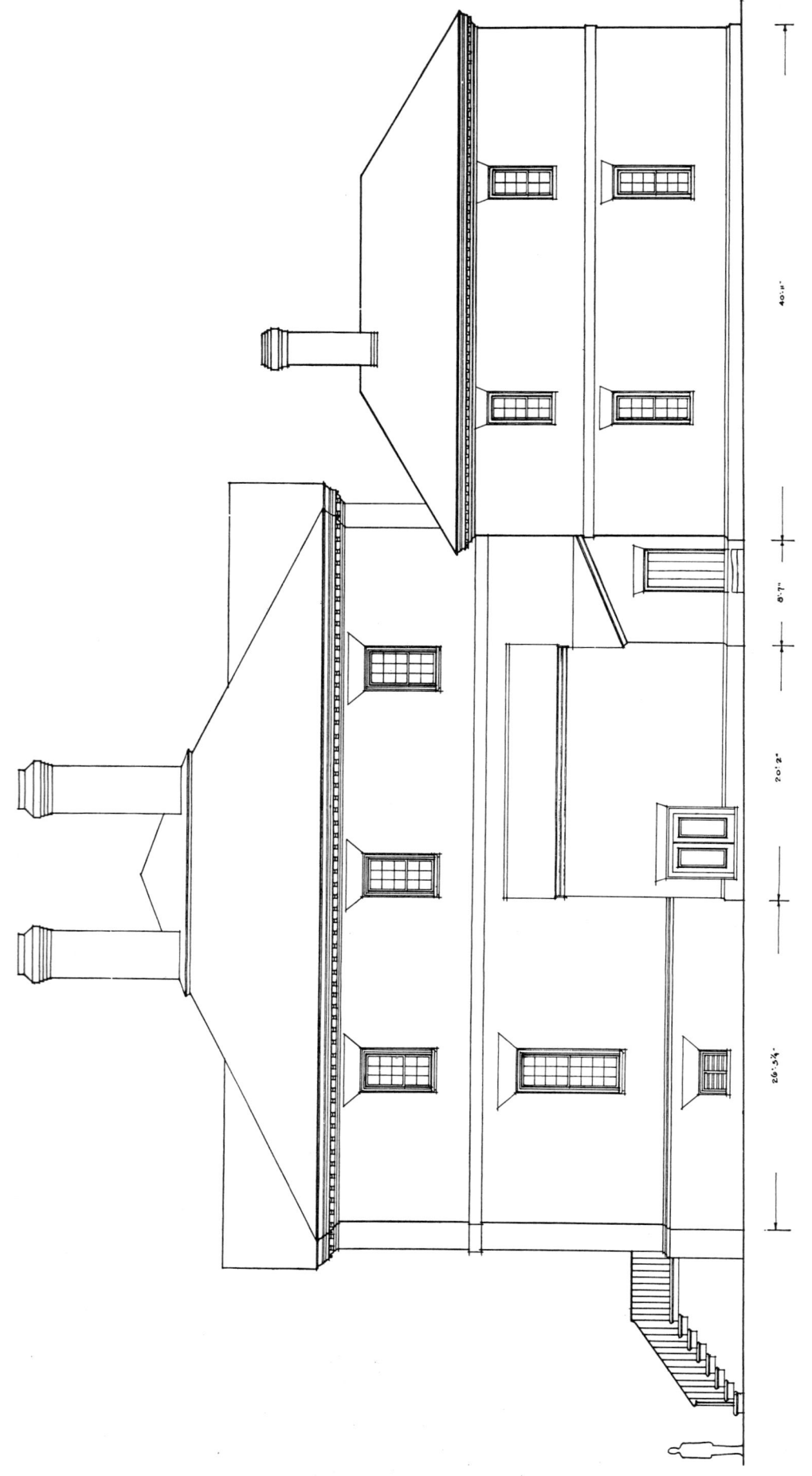

BLANDFIELD, RESTORED WEST ELEVATION
Scale, 3/32 in. to the foot

Menokin

MENOKIN, RICHMOND COUNTY

Menokin

RICHMOND COUNTY

1769

Six miles west of the town of Warsaw, near an old water mill bearing the same name, is Menokin, one of the most interesting of the late Georgian houses in Virginia. Little known, this house is full of architectural interest. In its decay it stands in very much the same form as when built by Colonel John Tayloe of Mount Airy, for his daughter Rebecca, who became the bride of Francis Lightfoot Lee in 1769. This statesman and patriot, son of Thomas Lee, was born at Stratford in 1734. In 1765 he was elected to the House of Burgesses and later was four times a member of the Continental Congress. He and Richard Henry Lee were the only two brothers to sign the Declaration of Independence. As no children came of his marriage to Rebecca Tayloe, the house was inherited by his nephew, Ludwell Lee, son of Richard Henry Lee.

In Menokin, the same materials as those in Mount Airy are used, and though the latter was larger in scale and more extensive in *parti*, the hand of the same builder is seen in both dwellings.

The house, the dimensions of which are only 42 by 44 feet, is so skilfully designed that its diminutive size is scarcely realized. Until recent years, two dependencies formed a court before the central building. After the War between the States when the kitchen was moved to one of the rooms within the house itself, the eastern building served several uses and was finally demolished. In size and design, it was the duplicate of the remaining one.

The exterior walls of the main house are now plastered. However, it is easy to see that this was not intended in the original scheme. The stone is nicely cut and laid and the joints are well pointed and of even width. The color, like that of the walls of Mount Airy, is a golden brown. Quoins, water-table and trim stone at Menokin are of the same material as the walls themselves and would lose in value were it not for the white plaster to create a contrast.

The water-table, a coarsely moulded member, runs around the four sides of the house and breaks out at the point where it meets the quoins. Below the water-table the stone of the corners consists of three large square projecting blocks. Above, the corners are quoined and are vigorously rusticated.

The front of the house is divided horizontally by two stone bands; one at the second-floor line and one at the sill line of the upper windows. On the other sides of the house this latter course is eliminated. Its presence on the north front creates a breadth which the opposite façade lacks.

As if to compensate for the narrow wood frames of the windows on both floors, the openings are faced with broad stone surrounds. Those on the first floor are made up of simple pier and lintel members, no mouldings being employed. On the north front the windows of the second floor, however, are exceptionally interesting. The design of the central window is simpler than that of the two on the corners, as only low plinths on the line of the sill receive the bolder moulded stone architrave. The flanking windows are surrounded with more richly moulded architraves which are interrupted by heavy quoins. The architraves mitre at the head and are received by heavy voussoirs that step up on either side of a projecting keystone.

Under a modern wooden porch a full cornice supported by carved consoles suggests a hood over the arched doorway. On either side of the opening are piers with moulded caps and bases, and though now covered with plaster, the form of their profile may be detected. A broad flat archivolt, the width of the piers, swings over the arch of the door and supports a key, carved with an archaic spray of flowers. In the basement windows a moulded plinth is supplied to receive the wide stone frame. A coarse keystone is also used in the arch above these openings.

The sash on both floors appears to be original. The muntins are lighter than those of contemporary work, but the mouldings are characteristic of late Georgian design. The double-valve door is original but the transom is modern. In the main cornice the modillions that it was designed to have are lacking and the woodwork has suffered from weathering.

The roof is a hip-on-hip, characteristic of the Rappahannock region. Its lower slope is pierced by two brick stacks which tower above the ridge and end in a simple capping. The roof in late years has been covered with sheet metal.

The walls of the dependency are of uncoursed rubble, as are the sides and south fronts of the main building. Its corners are of semi-dressed random blocks together with the base and string course. The lower windows are spanned by flat arches containing delicate dressed keystones. The key over the door is fluted and is contained in a semi-circular arch.

In character the dependency is very much more refined than the house. Its cornice is negligible and the roof pitch is exceedingly low. The stone chimneys are very narrow in end elevation, but widen on the ridge. They are topped with moulded stone caps. Although naïve, the building is very attractive. Its interior has woodwork of unusual merit, including a fine Chippendale stairway.

In its unrestored state, Menokin retains more ante-bellum charm than any of its more fortunate neighbors. Most of the original woodwork of the interior remains in place, and while not of great distinction, it makes the house a complete exemplar of the period. This is unusual in a region where so many interiors have been destroyed or exteriors altered.

In the restoration presented herewith, the missing dependency has been replaced and the wooden porch removed. Modillions have been reinstated in the cornice. The detail shows half the front of the house as it exists, with plaster covering the ashlar. The porch is removed in order to show the architecture of the front door in full.

Menokin

SOUTHWEST CORNER OF MAIN HOUSE

Men

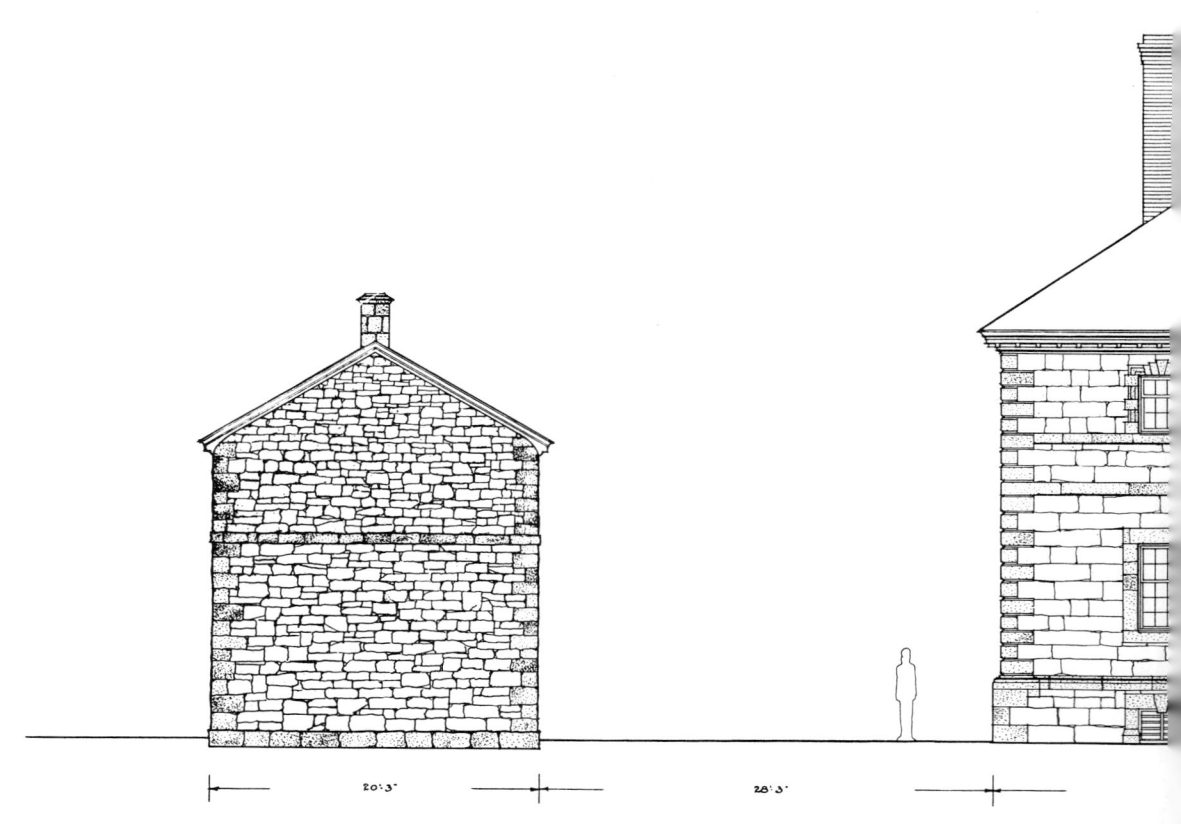

RESTORED FRONT EL[EVATION]
Scale, $\tfrac{3}{32}$ in. to the

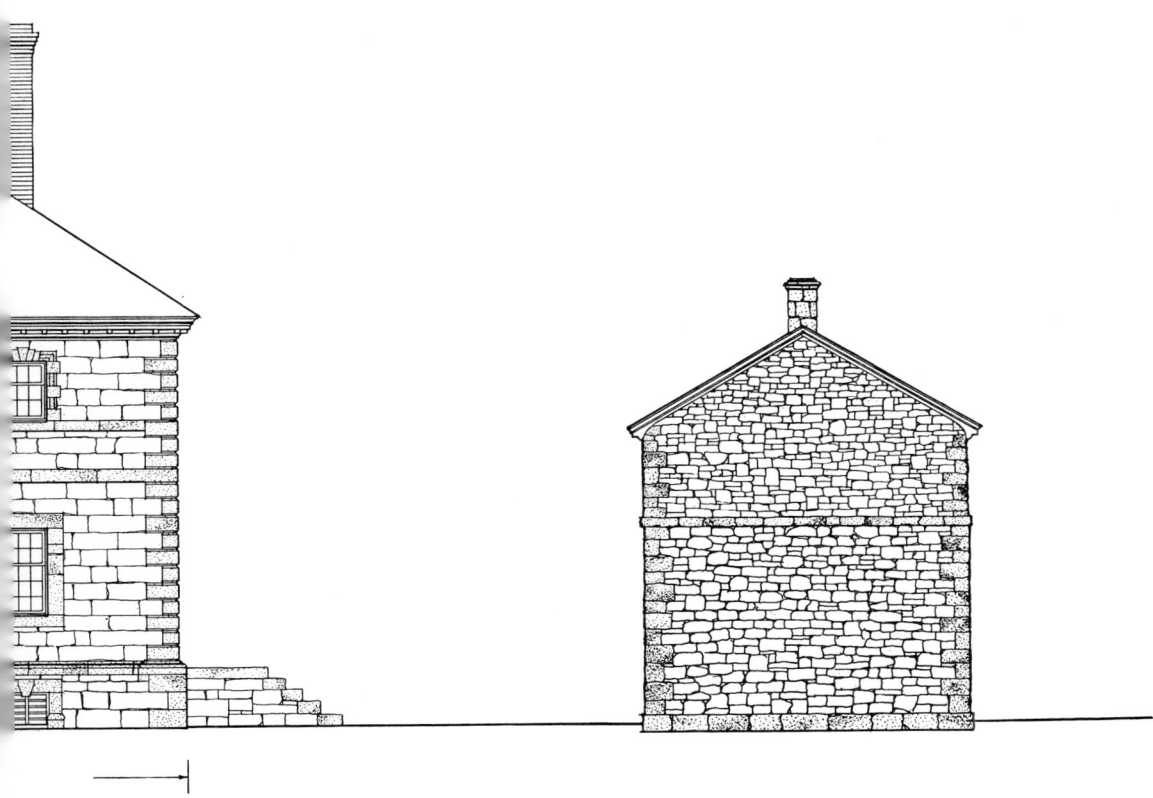

MAIN HOUSE FROM THE NORTHWEST

DETAIL OF FRONT ELEVATION
Scale, ¼ in. to the foot

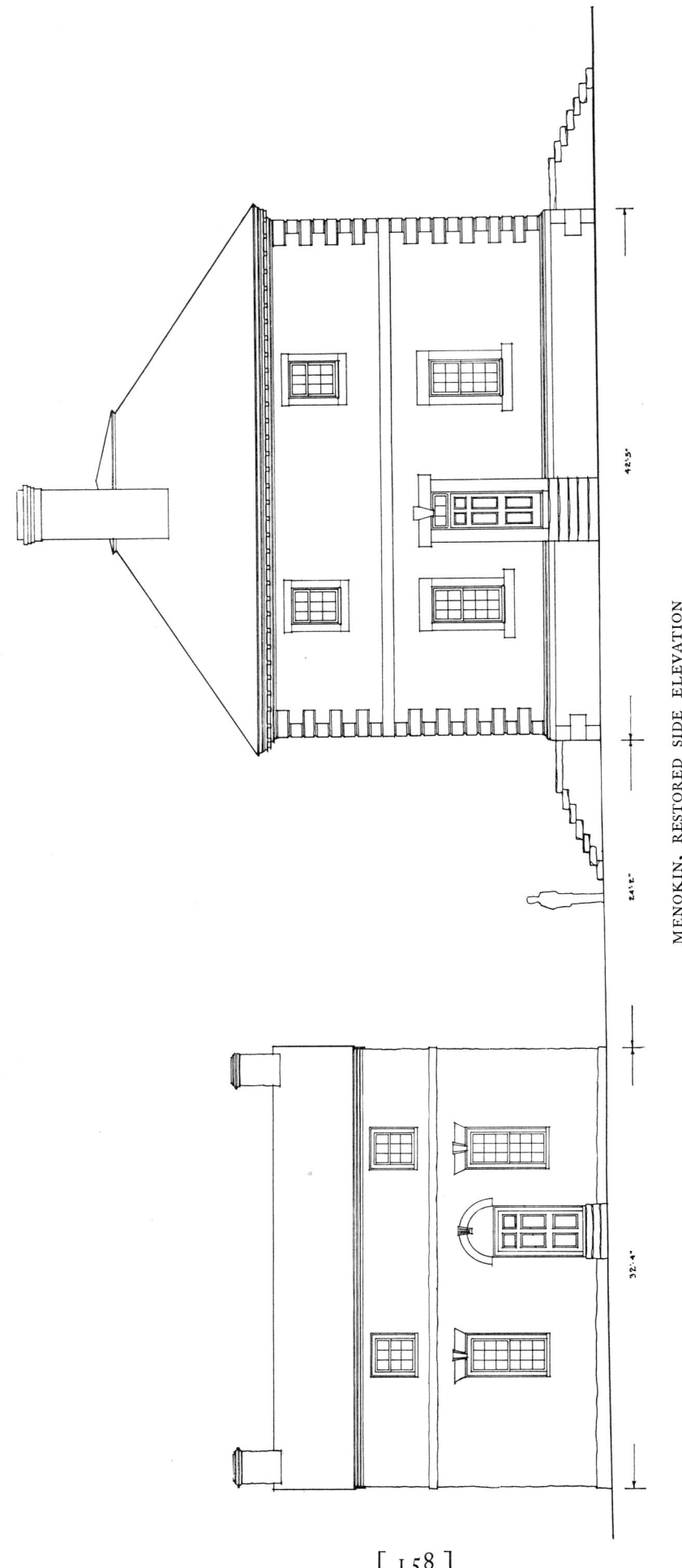

MENOKIN, RESTORED SIDE ELEVATION
Scale, 3/32 in. to the foot

Menokin

DOORWAY AND BRACKETED ENTABLATURE UNDER LATER PORCH

DEPENDENCY FROM THE SOUTHEAST

Details of Profiles

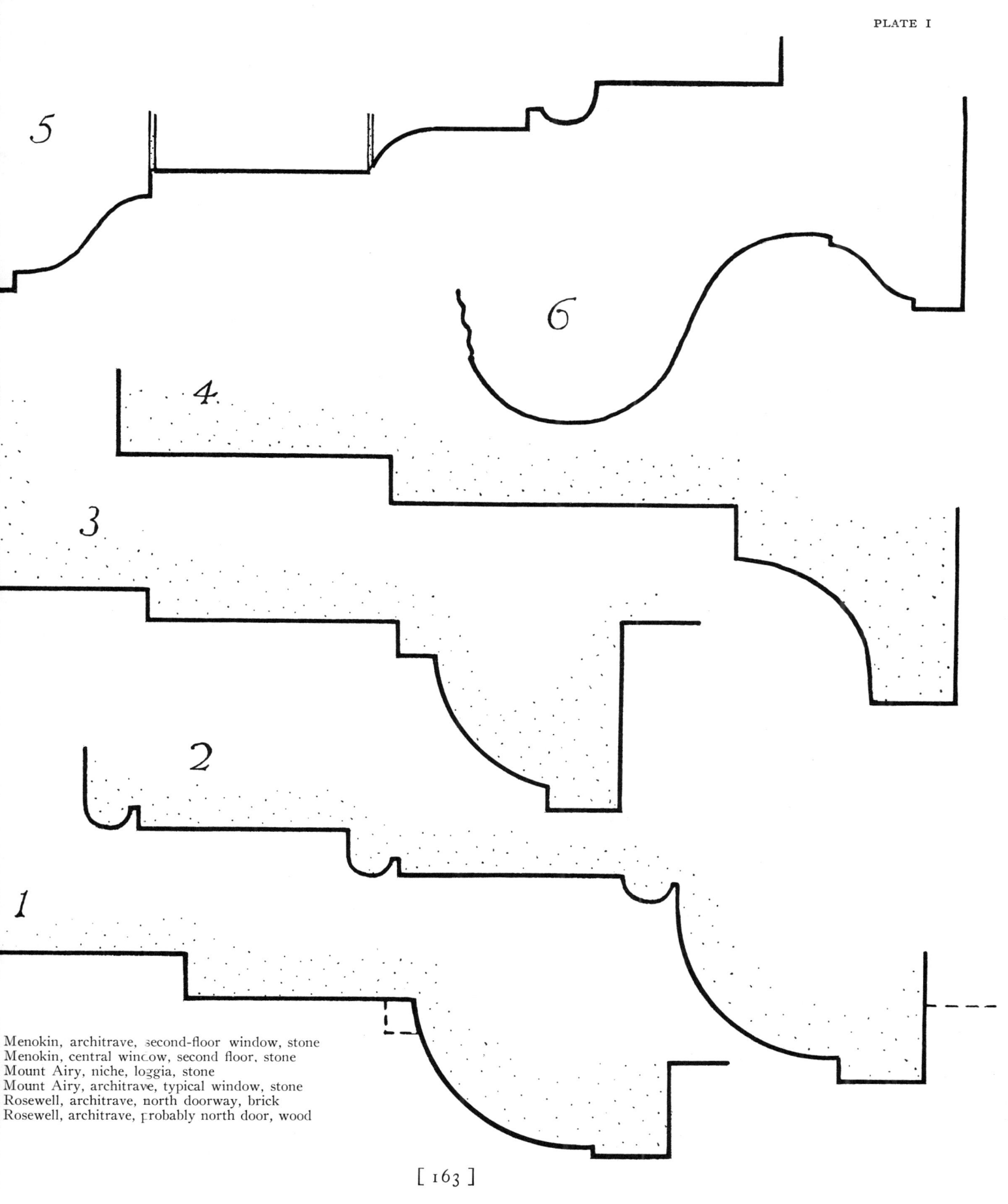

1. Menokin, architrave, second-floor window, stone
2. Menokin, central window, second floor, stone
3. Mount Airy, niche, loggia, stone
4. Mount Airy, architrave, typical window, stone
5. Rosewell, architrave, north doorway, brick
6. Rosewell, architrave, probably north door, wood

PLATE 2

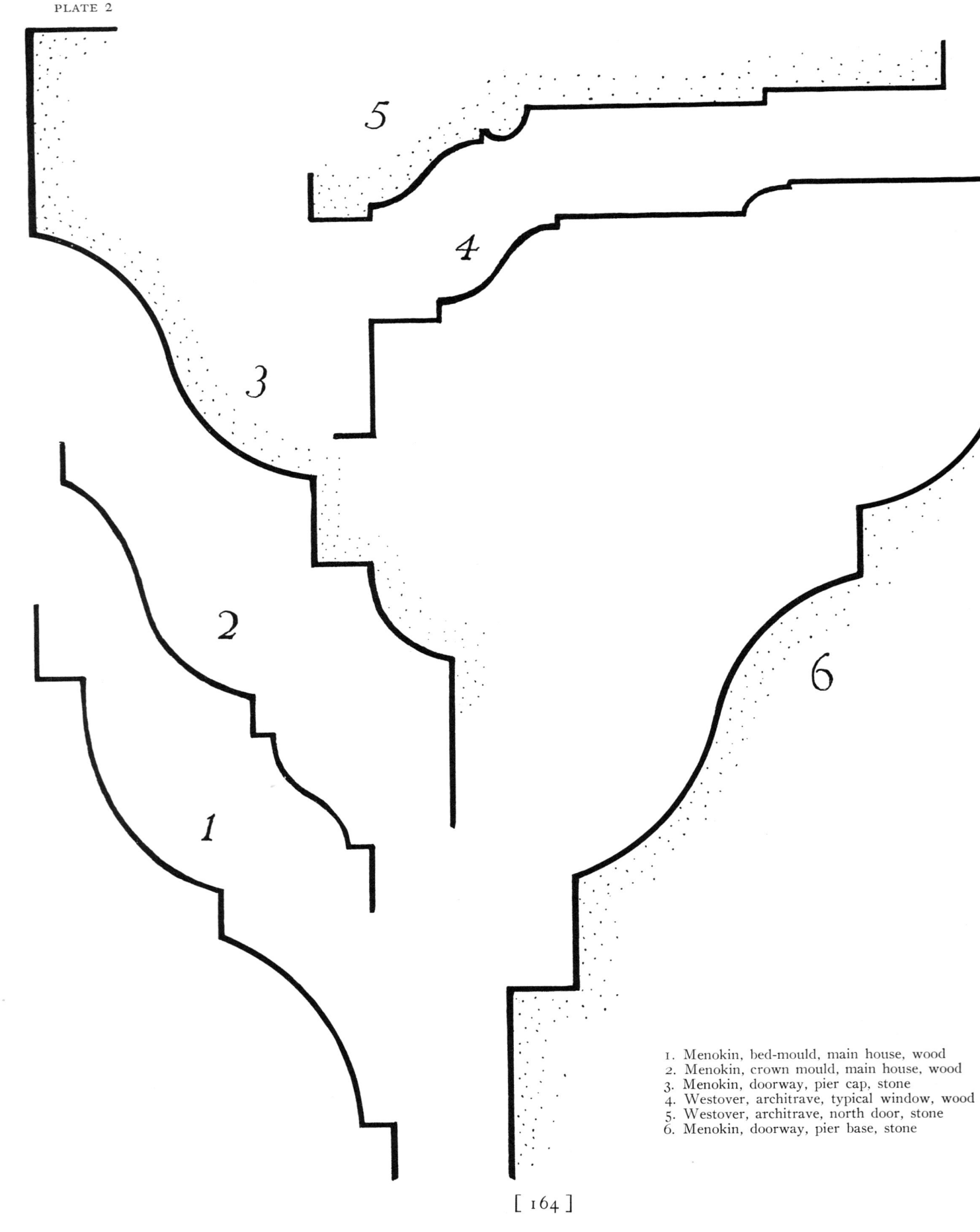

1. Menokin, bed-mould, main house, wood
2. Menokin, crown mould, main house, wood
3. Menokin, doorway, pier cap, stone
4. Westover, architrave, typical window, wood
5. Westover, architrave, north door, stone
6. Menokin, doorway, pier base, stone

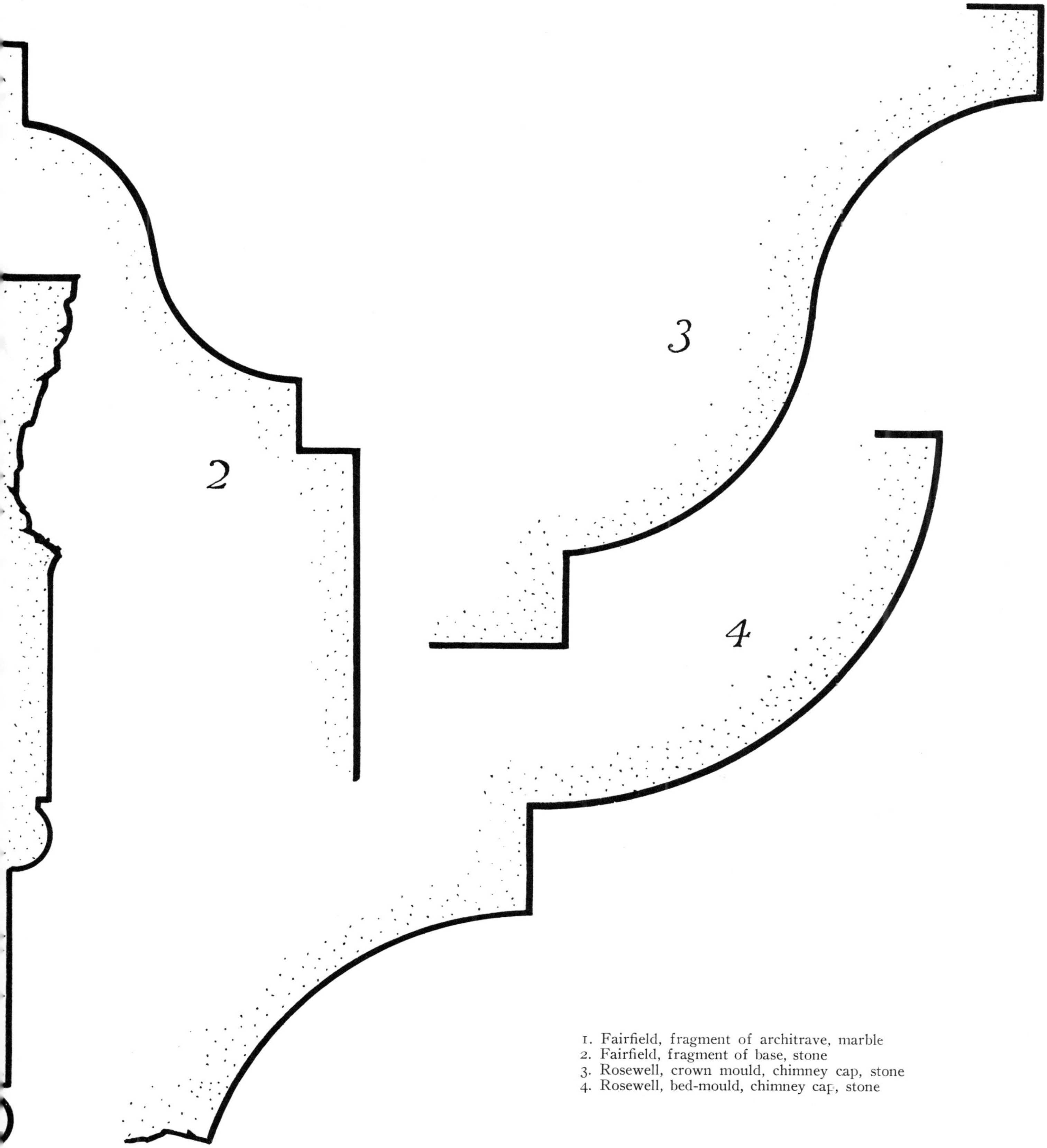

PLATE 3

1. Fairfield, fragment of architrave, marble
2. Fairfield, fragment of base, stone
3. Rosewell, crown mould, chimney cap, stone
4. Rosewell, bed-mould, chimney cap, stone

PLATE 4

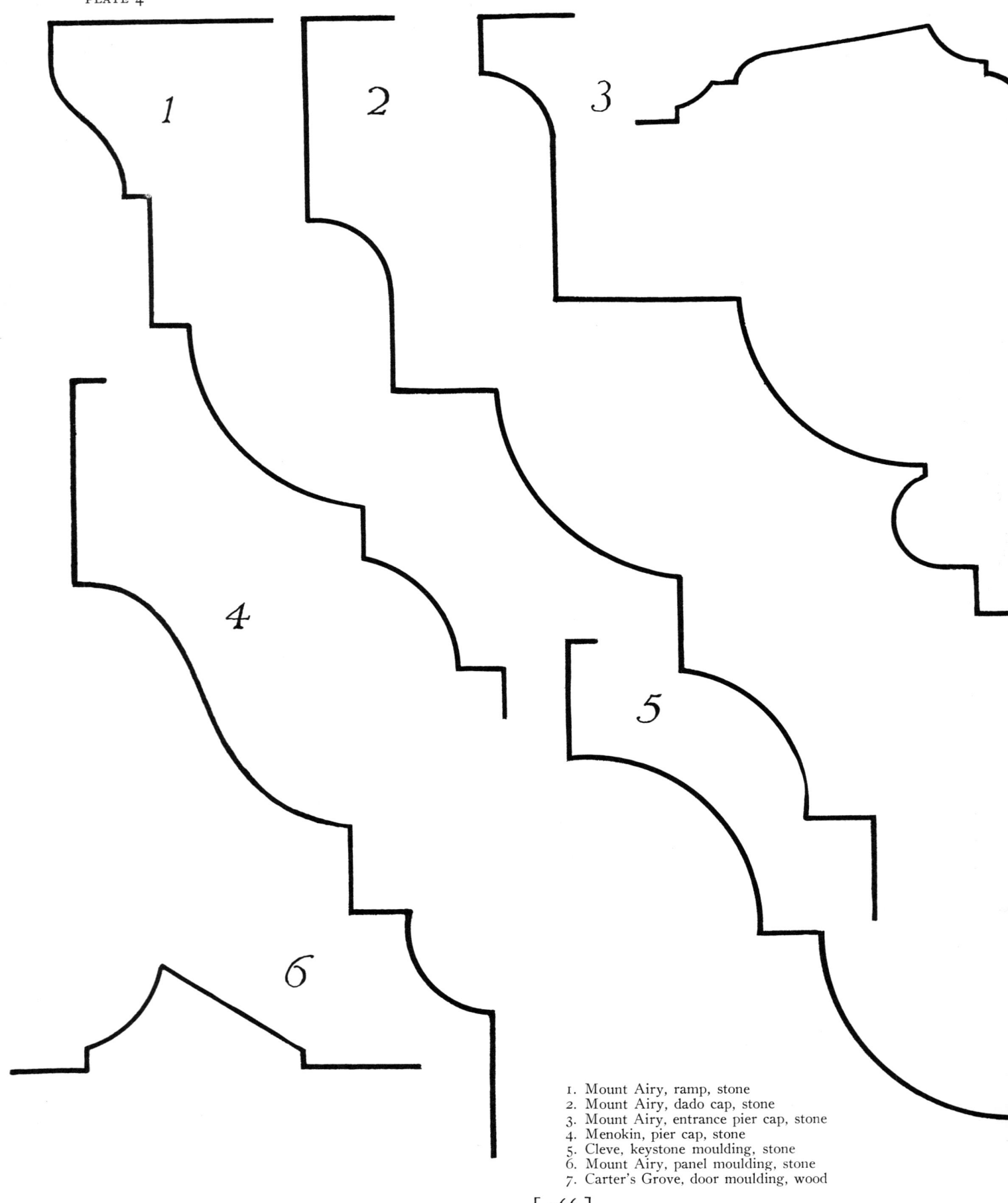

1. Mount Airy, ramp, stone
2. Mount Airy, dado cap, stone
3. Mount Airy, entrance pier cap, stone
4. Menokin, pier cap, stone
5. Cleve, keystone moulding, stone
6. Mount Airy, panel moulding, stone
7. Carter's Grove, door moulding, wood

[166]

PLATE 5

1. Westover, pilaster base, north doorway, stone
2. Rosewell, pilaster base, south doorway, stone
3. Mount Airy, pier base, north doorway, stone
4. Menokin, plinth, basement windows, stone

PLATE 6

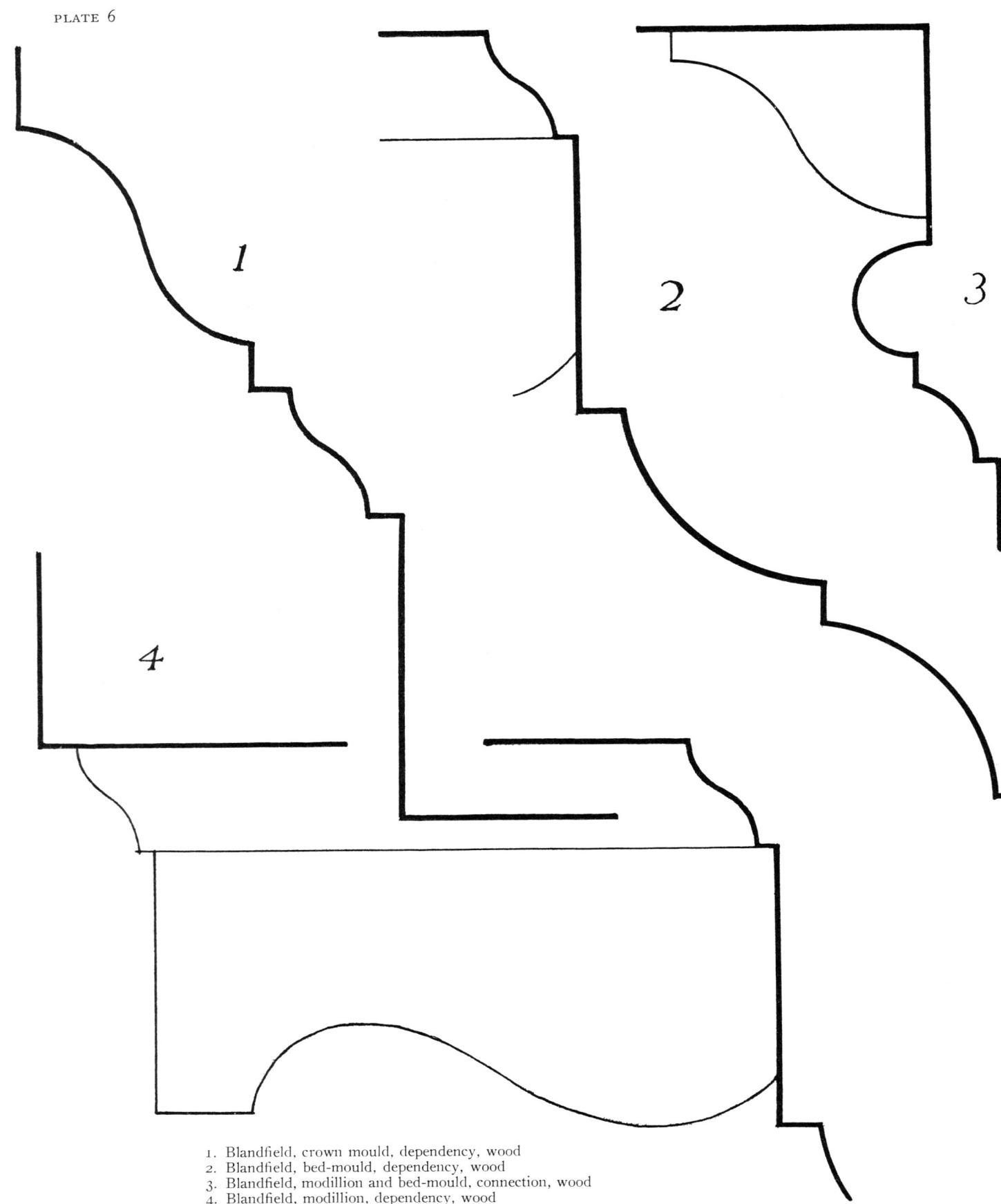

1. Blandfield, crown mould, dependency, wood
2. Blandfield, bed-mould, dependency, wood
3. Blandfield, modillion and bed-mould, connection, wood
4. Blandfield, modillion, dependency, wood

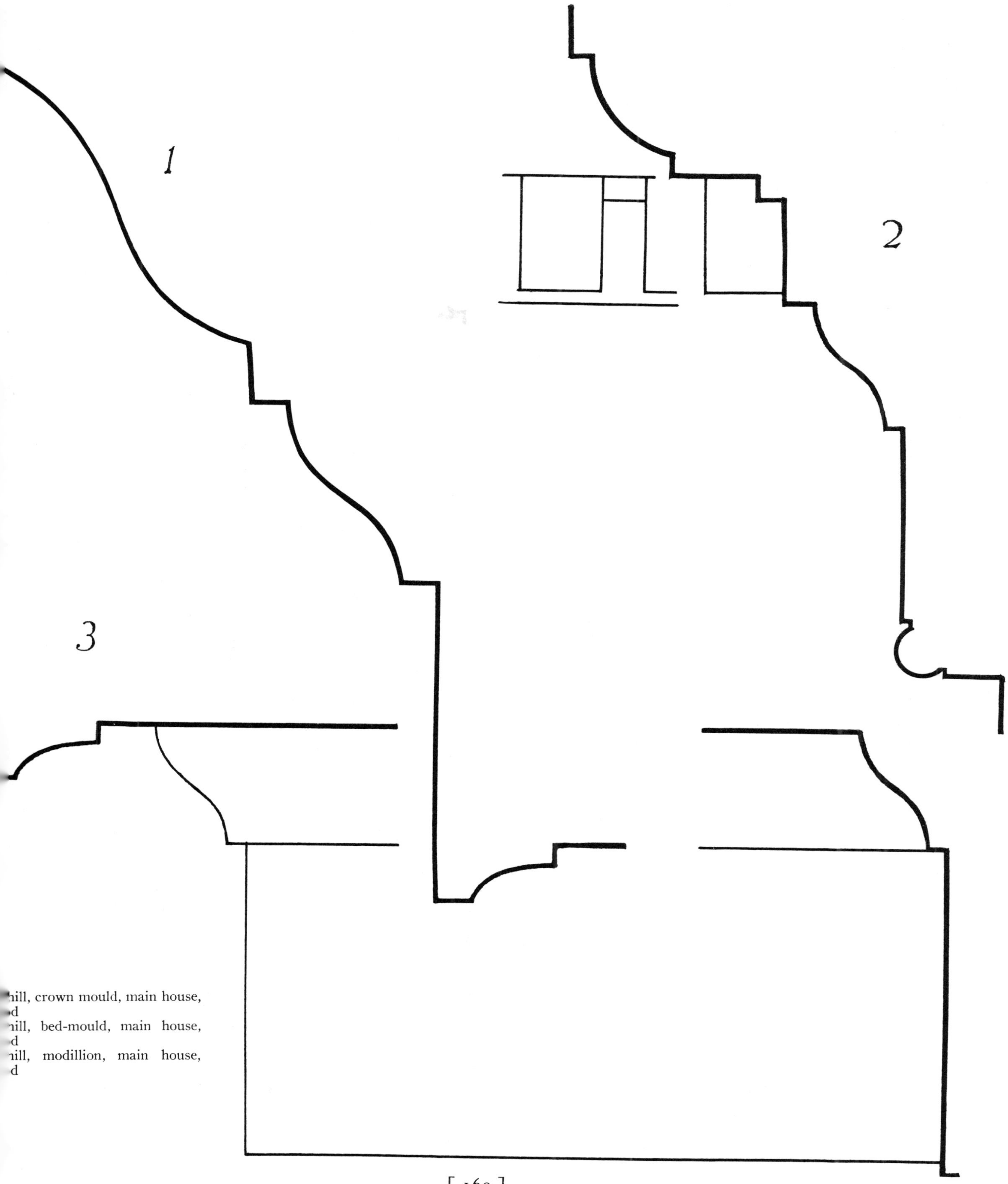

PLATE 7

hill, crown mould, main house,
d
hill, bed-mould, main house,
d
hill, modillion, main house,
d

[169]

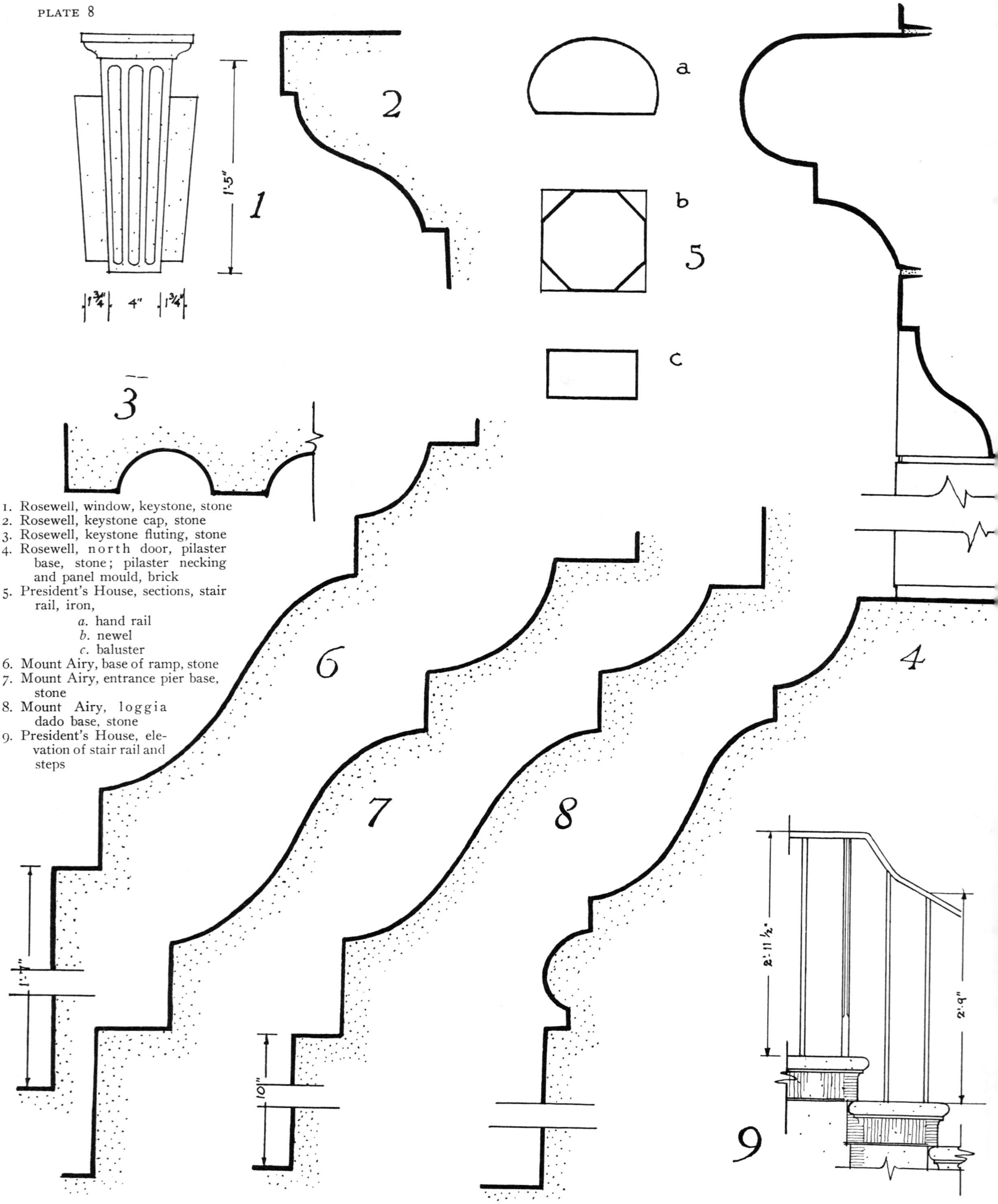

PLATE 8

1. Rosewell, window, keystone, stone
2. Rosewell, keystone cap, stone
3. Rosewell, keystone fluting, stone
4. Rosewell, north door, pilaster base, stone; pilaster necking and panel mould, brick
5. President's House, sections, stair rail, iron,
    a. hand rail
    b. newel
    c. baluster
6. Mount Airy, base of ramp, stone
7. Mount Airy, entrance pier base, stone
8. Mount Airy, loggia dado base, stone
9. President's House, elevation of stair rail and steps

[170]

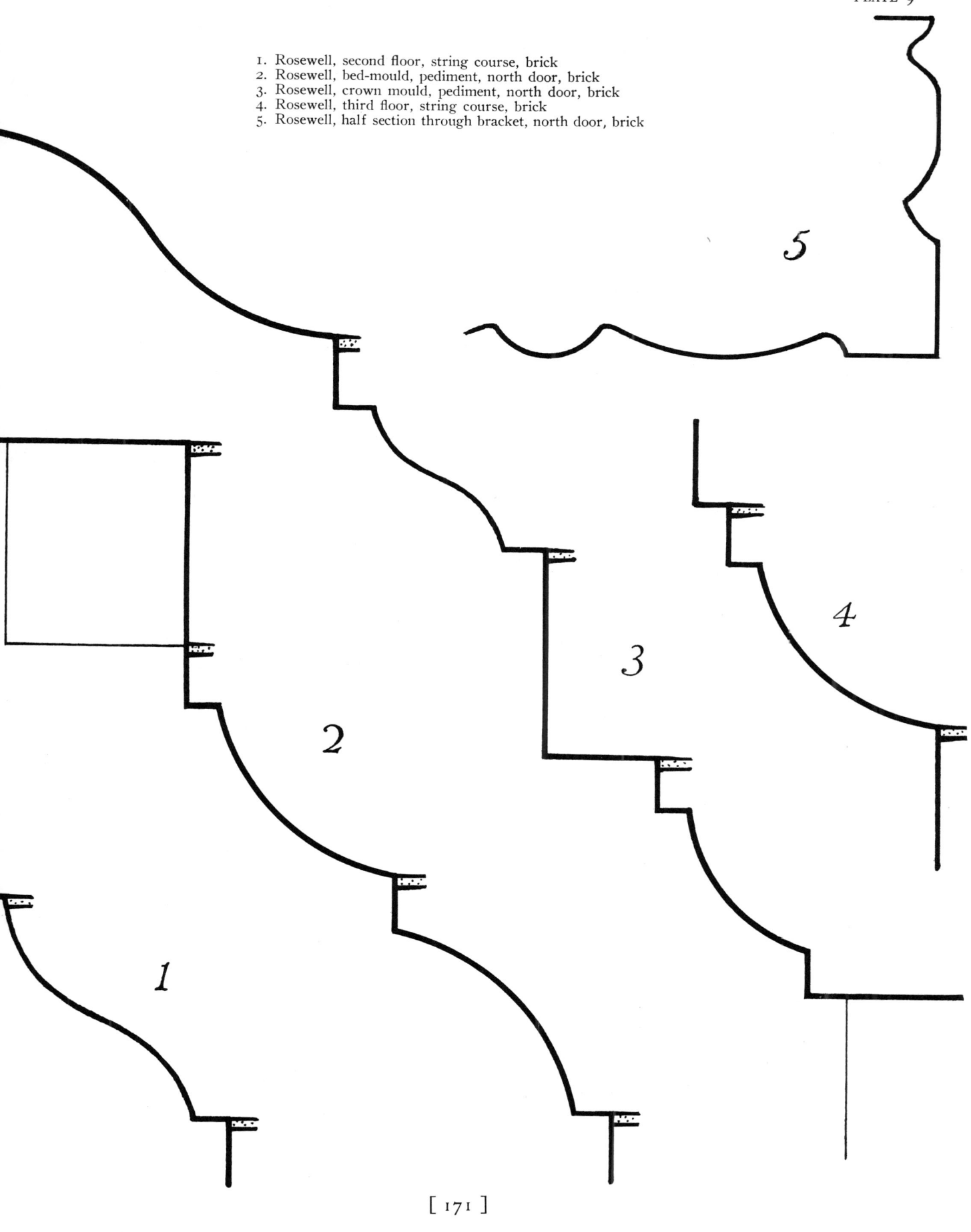

1. Rosewell, second floor, string course, brick
2. Rosewell, bed-mould, pediment, north door, brick
3. Rosewell, crown mould, pediment, north door, brick
4. Rosewell, third floor, string course, brick
5. Rosewell, half section through bracket, north door, brick

PLATE 10

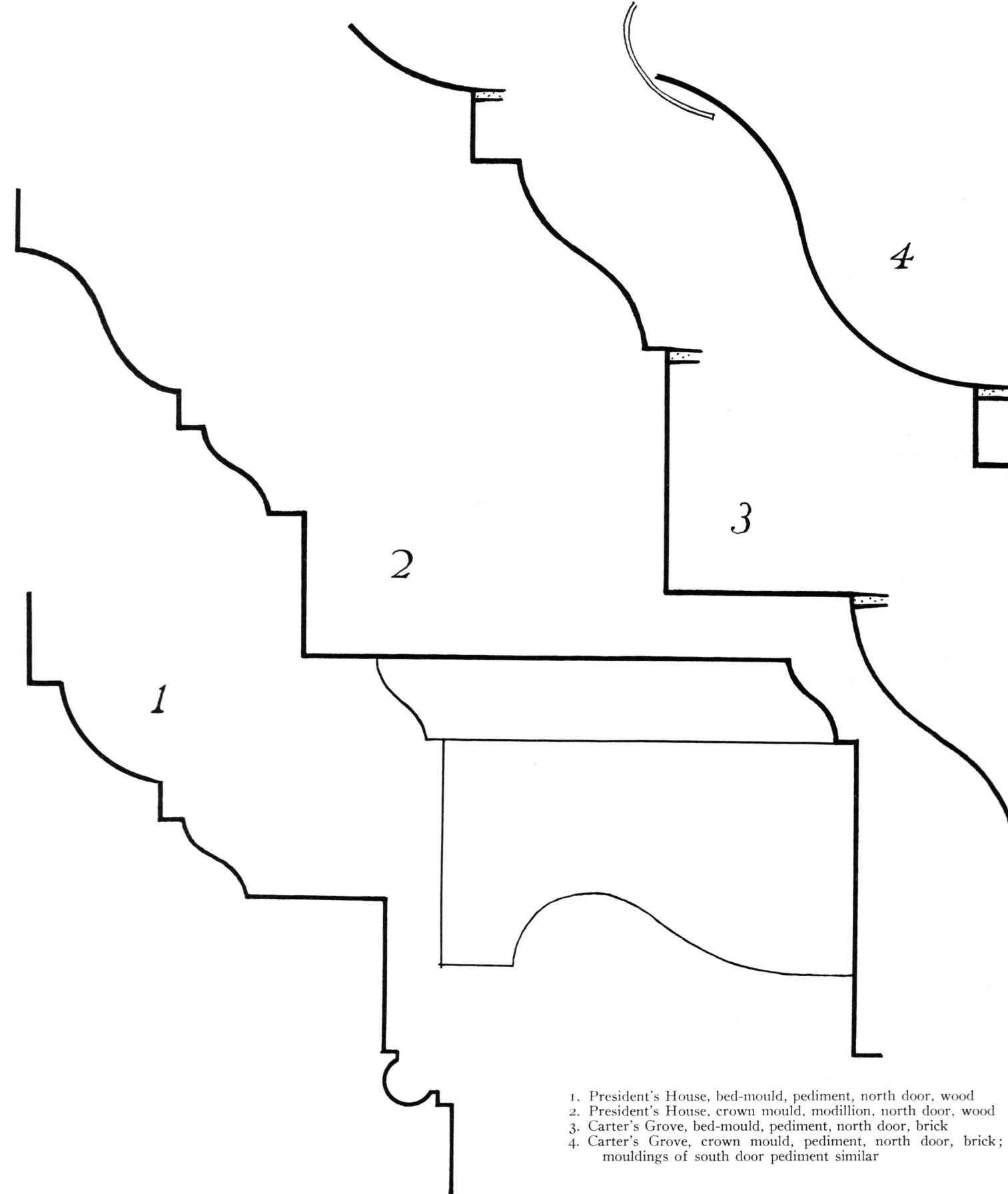

1. President's House, bed-mould, pediment, north door, wood
2. President's House, crown mould, modillion, north door, wood
3. Carter's Grove, bed-mould, pediment, north door, brick
4. Carter's Grove, crown mould, pediment, north door, brick; mouldings of south door pediment similar

[172]

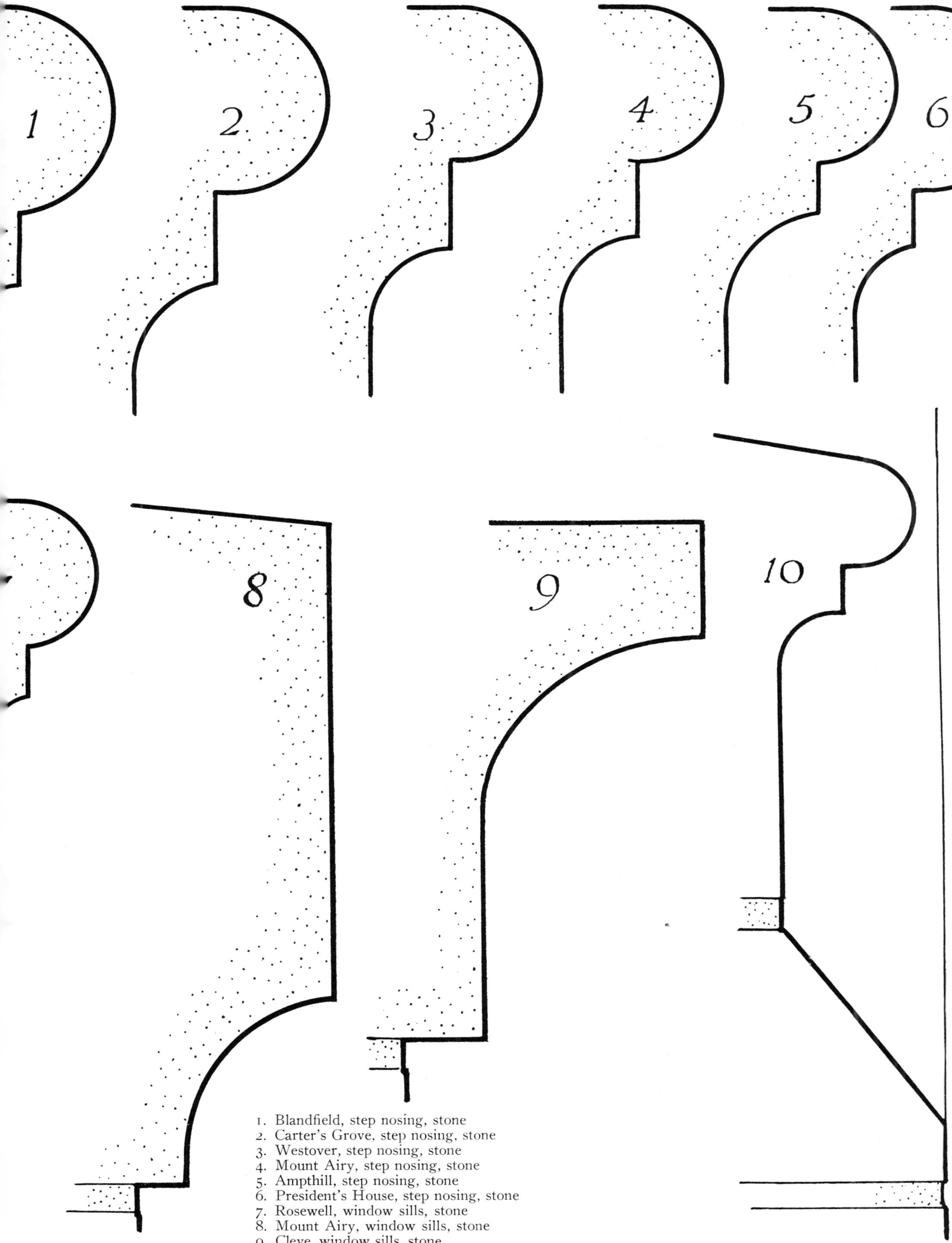

1. Blandfield, step nosing, stone
2. Carter's Grove, step nosing, stone
3. Westover, step nosing, stone
4. Mount Airy, step nosing, stone
5. Ampthill, step nosing, stone
6. President's House, step nosing, stone
7. Rosewell, window sills, stone
8. Mount Airy, window sills, stone
9. Cleve, window sills, stone
10. Westover, window sills, wood; brick wash at bottom of sill on first-floor and second-floor windows, as at President's House

PLATE 12

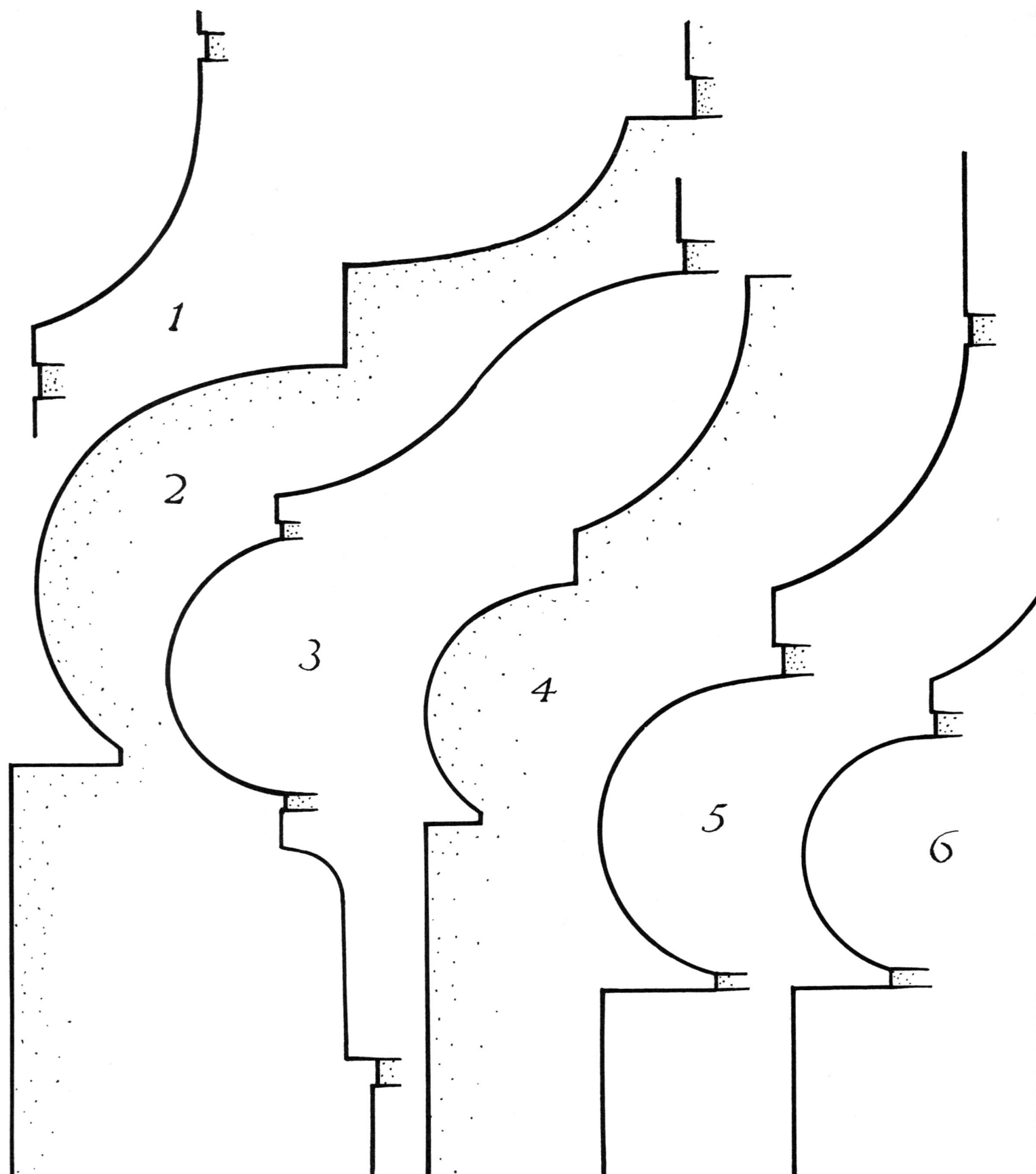

1. Blandfield, water-table, dependency, brick
2. Menokin, water-table, main house, stone
3. Rosewell, water-table, main house, brick
4. Cleve, water-table, main house, stone
5. Blandfield, water-table, main house, brick
6. Wilton, water-table, main house, brick

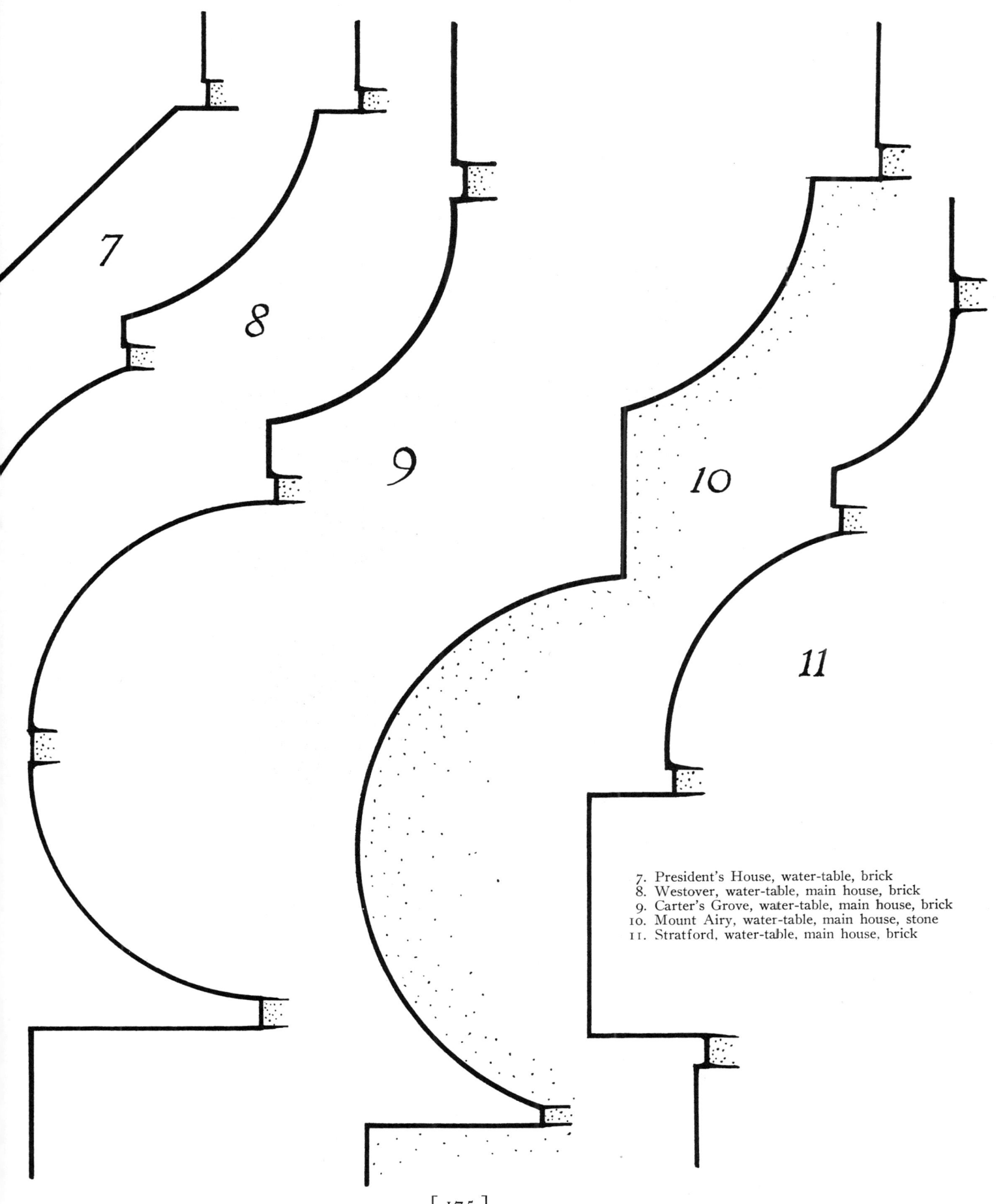

7. President's House, water-table, brick
8. Westover, water-table, main house, brick
9. Carter's Grove, water-table, main house, brick
10. Mount Airy, water-table, main house, stone
11. Stratford, water-table, main house, brick

DETAIL OF BRICKWORK AT WILTON

Brick Sizes

Thoroughgood House   2 x 4 x 8½
     4 courses equal 11½"

Bacon's Castle   2⅝ x 4 x 8½
     4 courses equal 1'-0"

Ampthill   2¼ x 3¾ x 8
     4 courses equal 11"
     2¾ x 3¾ x 7½
     4 courses equal 1'-0¼" in dependencies

President's House   2⅝ x 4¼ x 9
     4 courses equal 1'-0"

Stratford   2¼ x 4⅛ x 7⅝
     5 courses equal 1'-0"

Westover   2⅜ x 3¾ x 8
     4 courses equal 11" (12" in wing)

Rosewell   2¼ x 4 x 8¼
     5 courses equal 1'-2"

Carter's Grove   2⅝ x 4 x 8½
     4 courses equal 1'-0"

Cleve   2¾ x 4 x 8½
     4 courses equal 1'-0¾" (5 joints)

Wilton   2⅛ x 3⅜ x 8
     4 courses equal 11"

Blandfield   3 x 4 x 9¼
     4 courses equal 1'-1½"
     2¾ x 4 x 9
     4 courses equal 1'-0½" in dependencies

A Comparison of Outline Plans

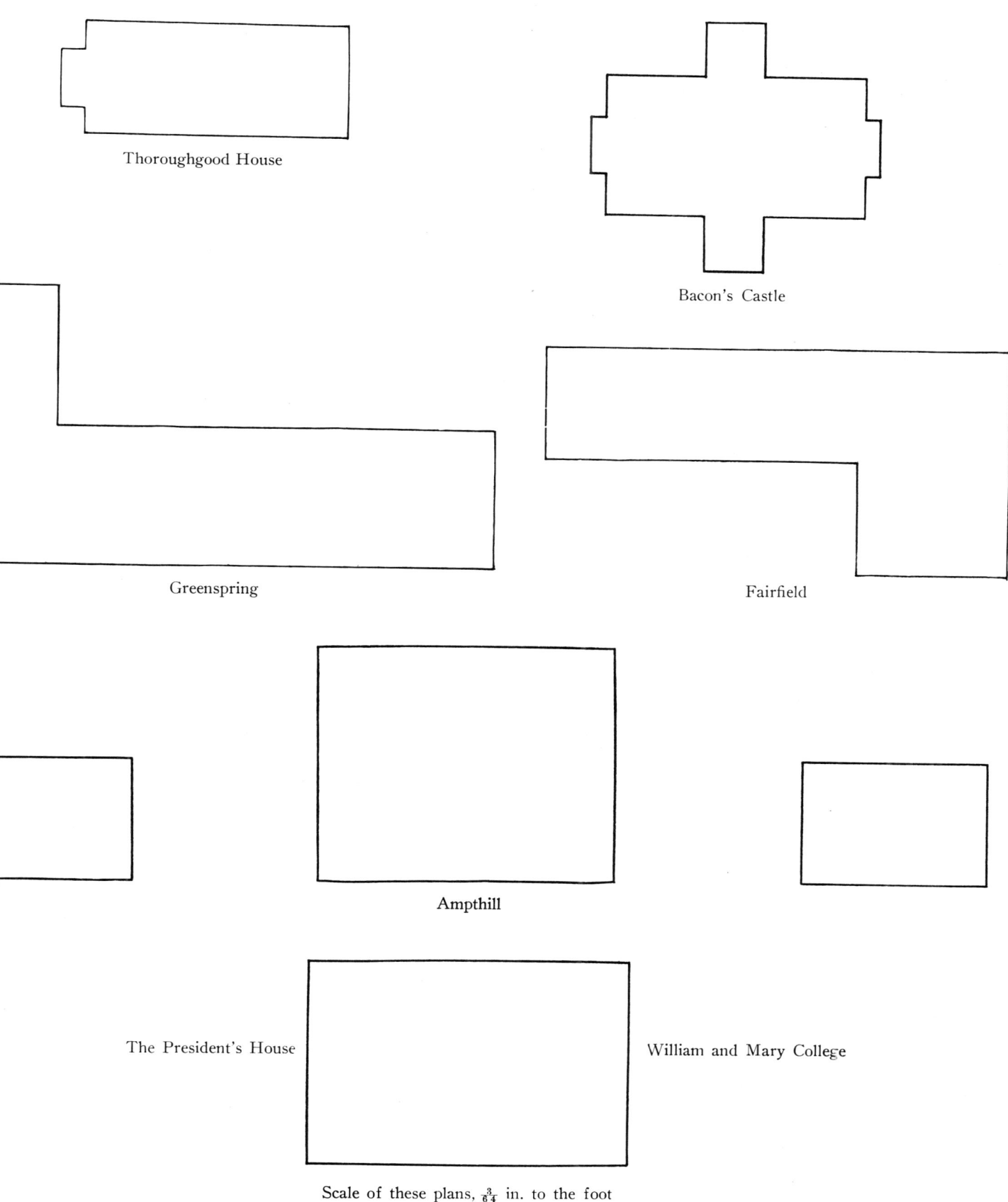

Scale of these plans, 3/64 in. to the foot

Stratford   Scale. $\tfrac{3}{128}$ in. to the foot (half the scale of the other plans)

[180]

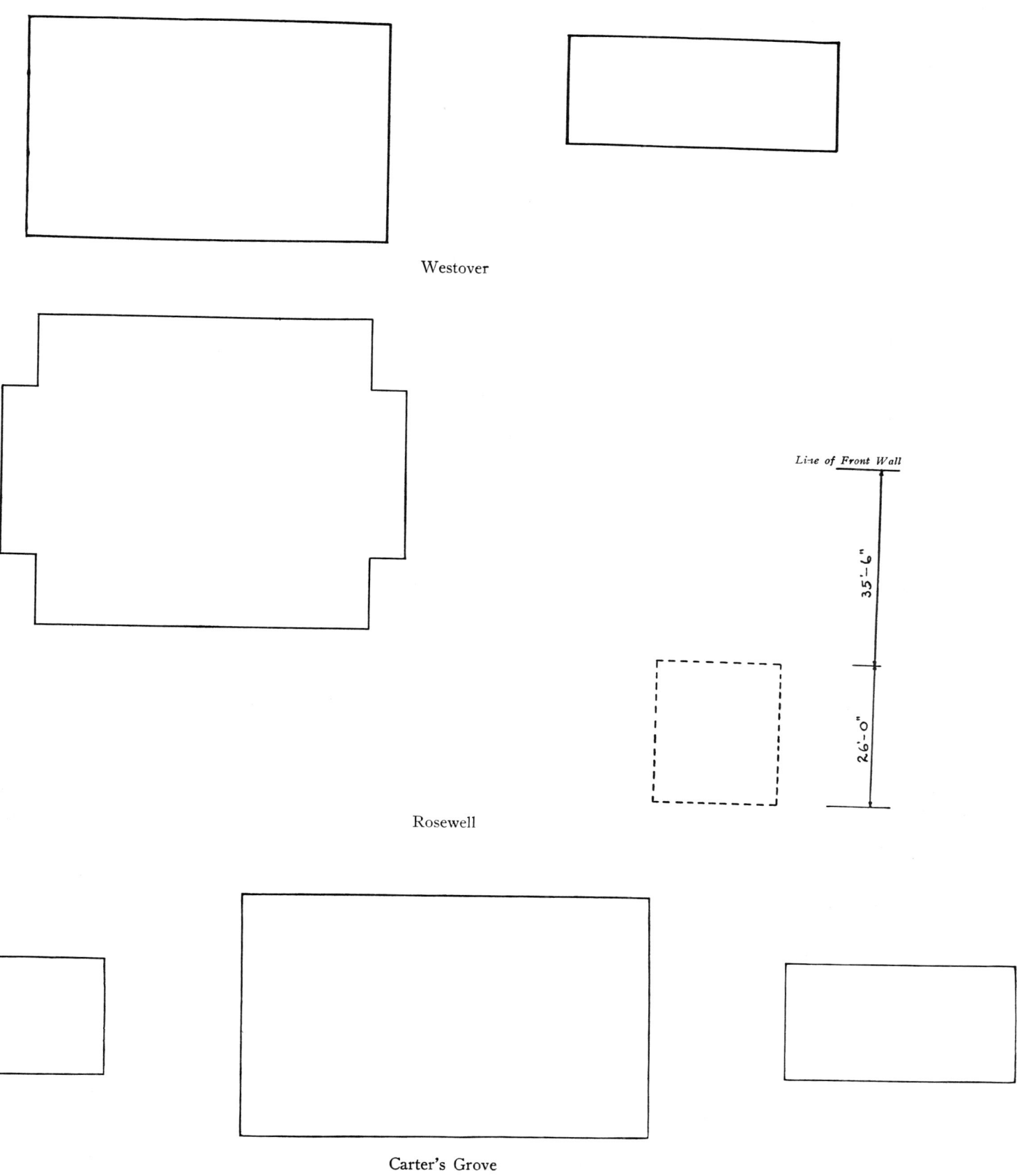

Westover

Rosewell

Carter's Grove

Scale of these plans, $\tfrac{3}{64}$ in. to the foot

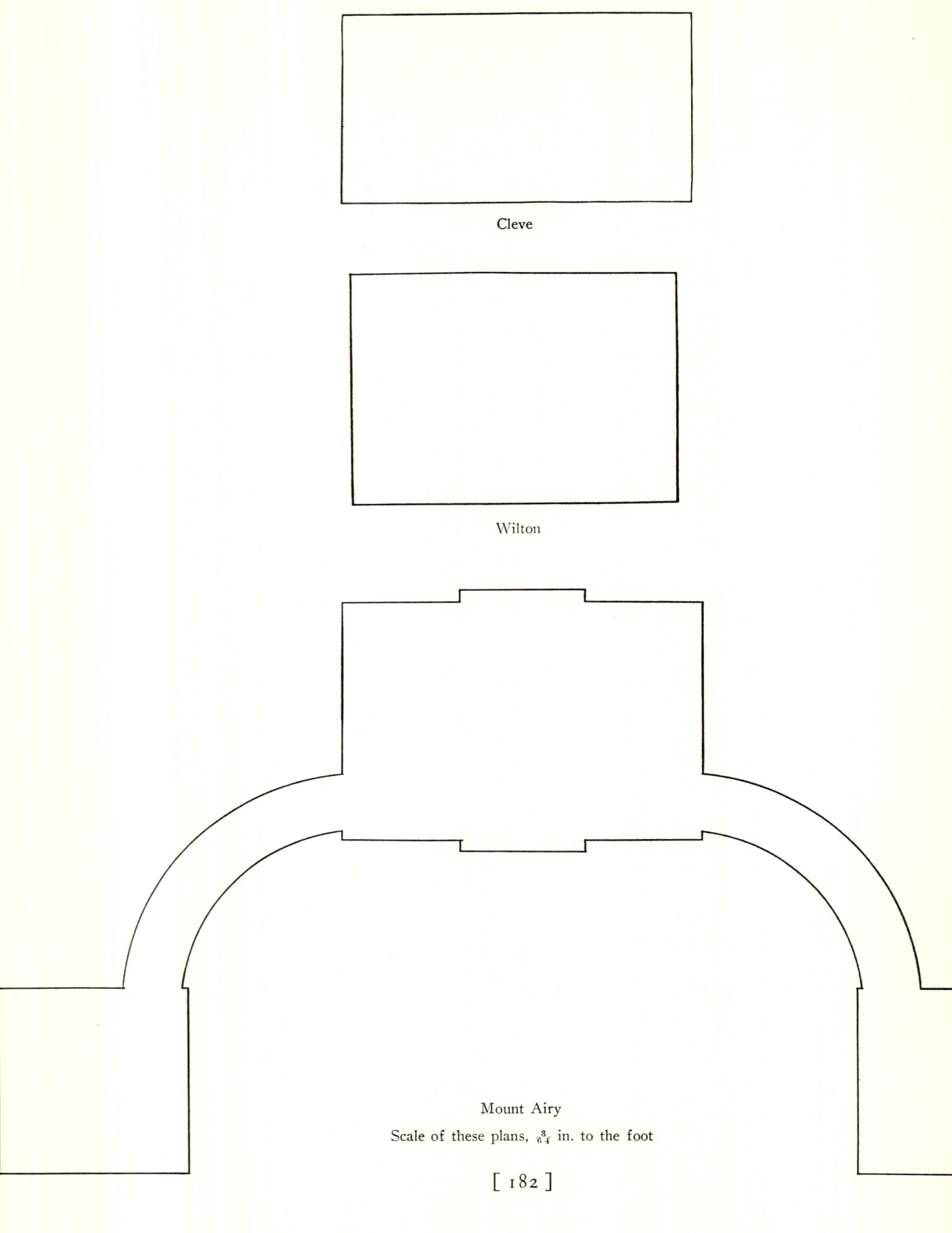

Cleve

Wilton

Mount Airy
Scale of these plans, $\frac{3}{64}$ in. to the foot

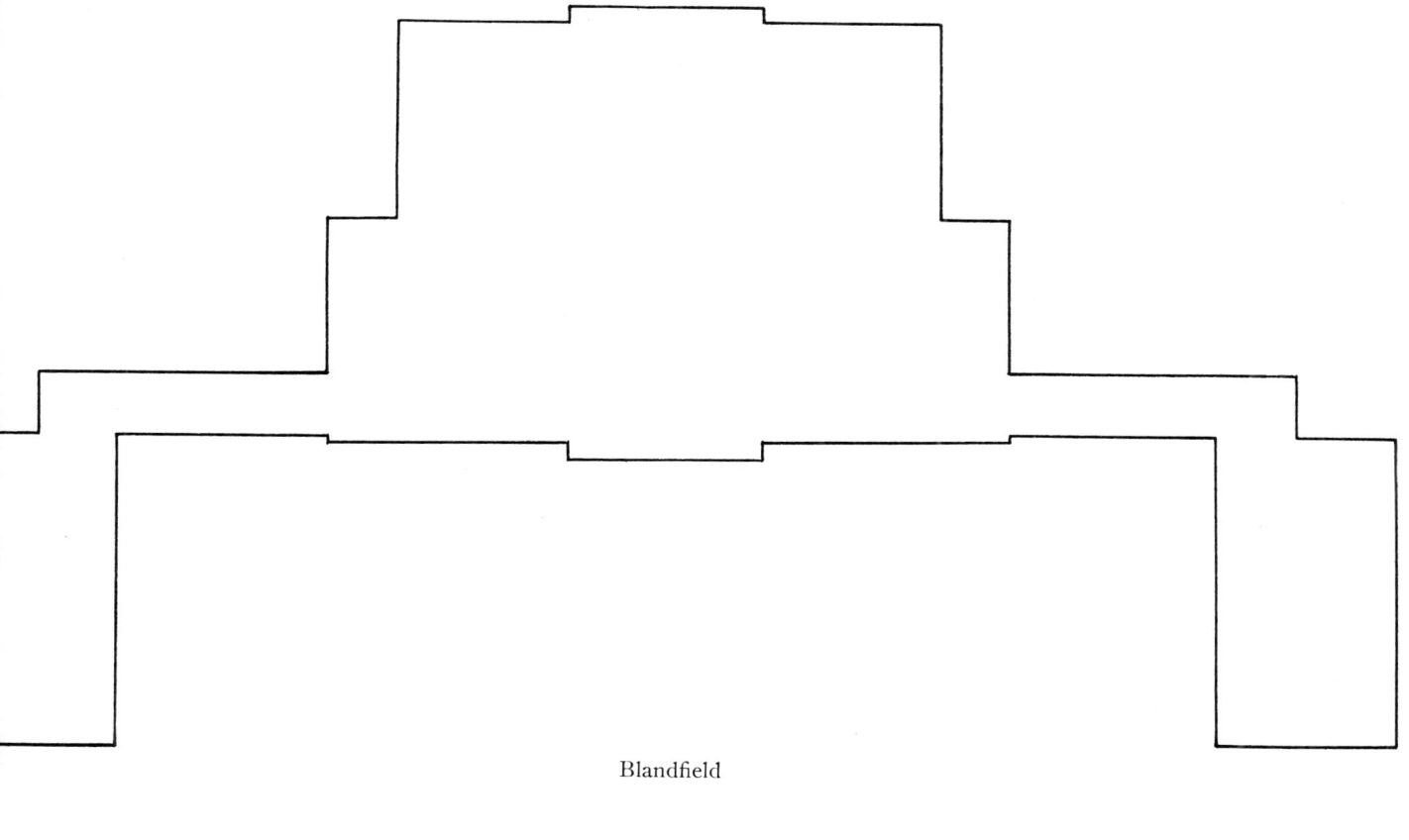

Blandfield

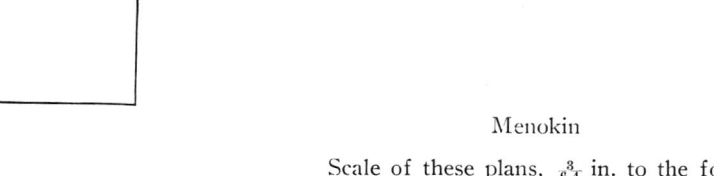

Menokin

Scale of these plans, $\frac{3}{64}$ in. to the foot

Glossary of Architectural Terms

Apron: An area of projecting brickwork or stonework below a window.
Architrave: The finish surrounding a door or window, or the lowest member of an entablature.
Archivolt: A moulded frame running over the faces of the voussoirs in an arch, or the inner contour of an arch.
Ashlar: A facing of squared stones.

Barge board: See verge board.
Bed-mould: The lower mouldings of a cornice.
Belt course: A projecting course or courses on the exterior of a building, usually at the floor or window sill line.
Bolection: In joinery, a moulding following the outside edge of a panel and projecting beyond the face of the frame in which the panel is held.

Clairvoyée: A screen of ironwork across a forecourt.
Clerestory: A portion of a roof raised with its vertical faces glazed to permit the entrance of light.
Clipped gable: A gable of which the apex is cut back in hipped-roof form.
Closer: A bat used at the end of a course of brick to allow the bond to end in a header or stretcher at the corner.
Composite: The most elaborate of the Classic Orders, using the elements of the Corinthian and Ionic Orders.
Console: A bracket of scroll form.
Corbel table: A projecting course supported on a range of brackets.
Corbelled parapet: A parapet supported on projecting courses or corbels.
Cove: A concave moulding approaching a quadrant in section.
Crown mould: See Cymatium.
Curvilinear gable: A gable of fantastic form laid out in geometric curves.

Cyma: A moulding, in section concave at one termination, and convex at the other.
Cymatium: The upper moulding of a cornice.

Dado: A plain or panelled field, defined at top and bottom by mouldings, that traverses the lower part of a wall surface.
Deck-on-hip: A flat roof surmounting a hip. See Hip.
Dentils: Oblong blocks spaced in a band to decorate a cornice.
Dependencies: The minor or flanking buildings of a composition.

Eared architrave (or *Crosset*): A lateral projection of the architrave mouldings of classic doors and windows at the extremities of the lintel or head.
End board: A board cut to the profile of a cornice or in some decorative form, that receives the cornice in a gable-end building.
English bond: A method of laying brick wherein one course is laid with stretchers and the next with headers, thus bonding the double thickness of brick together.
Entablature: An assembly of three parts of a Classic order, cornice, frieze, and architrave, forming the member carried on the column.

Facia: A flat broad member used in a cornice or other moulded part.
Filet: A narrow flat band that separates and defines mouldings.
Finial: A terminating ornament used on the apex of gables, pediments, roofs, etc.
Flashing: Strips of lead, or other metal, worked into masonry or roofing, around string courses, dormers or other projecting features, to prevent leakage.
Flat arch: A series of wedge-shaped stones or

Glossary of Architectural Terms

bricks over an opening which, though simulating the appearance of a lintel, performs the arch function.

Flemish Bond: A method of laying brick wherein headers and stretchers alternate in each course and vertically headers are placed over stretchers to form a bond and give a cross pattern.

Fluting: The surface of a pilaster or column which is enriched with vertical channelling.

Forecourt: The area before a building, in a formal composition, which is enclosed by flanking buildings or walls.

Frieze: The portion of the entablature between the architrave and cornice.

Gambrel: A roof having its slope broken by an obtuse angle.

Gauging: Brick selected for color and rubbed to a smooth surface on all faces. Used for decorative purposes.

Gazebo: A cupola; a summer-house.

Glazed brick: Header brick bearing a gray or green transparent glaze applied to the end.

Grille: A grating or screen, usually of wood in this district, though occasionally of iron.

Head (window): Top of window; similarly of arch and of door.

Header: End of brick; a brick laid across the thickness of a wall.

Hip: The external angle in which adjacent roofs meet each other; a roof that slopes back equally from each side of a building.

Impost: A horizontal member from the top of which springs an arch.

Jamb: The reveal or lining of a doorway or other aperture.

Kingpost: The middle post of a truss which supports the tie beam.

Label mould: In Gothic architecture, the drip moulding of an arch or lintel.

Leading: The method employed previous to the use of wood muntins in sash to secure the glass in casements by the means of narrow lead strips.

Lights: Window panes.

Lintel: The horizontal top piece of a window or door opening.

Loggia: A covered gallery or portico.

Lozenge lights: Diamond-shaped quarries used in leaded glazing.

Lugs: That part of a window sill or door sill which is carried beyond the opening into the masonry wall.

Modillion: An ornamental block, applied to the underside of the projecting members of a cornice.

Mullion: A narrow wood or stone division between window openings.

Muntin: The horizontal or vertical members in sash, used to divide the glass. The horizontals are sometimes called bars.

Necking: The horizontal moulding which separates the capital of a column or pilaster from the shaft.

Neo-Classic: The revived use of Classic forms in the eighteenth and nineteenth centuries; the name of a style of architecture pertaining to the Classic Revival.

Ogee: A moulding, in section concave in one termination and convex at the other. See Cyma.

Orangery: A hot-house; a conservatory.

Overthrow: Ornamental ironwork spanning a gateway.

Ovolo: A convex moulding, approaching a quadrant in section.

Palladian motive: The arrangement of an arch flanked by lower square-headed openings and separated from them by columns or piers, which was much used by the architect Palladio.

Parapet: A low wall along a roof or terrace, used as a protection or decoration.

Parterre: A flower garden having the beds disposed in some formal form or pattern.

Parti: Scheme.

Pavilion: A projecting motive on a façade to give architectural emphasis.

Pediment: A crowning motive of pavilions, doorways or other architectural features, usually of

Glossary of Architectural Terms

low triangular form, sometimes broken in the centre to receive an ornament, and sometimes of segmental, elliptical or serpentine form.

Pier: A square supporting member; also the wall space between windows or other apertures.

Pilasters: A flat form of a column applied to a wall.

Plate: The timber in a roof which rests on the walls of a building and receives the roof rafters.

Pleasaunce: A retired garden.

Plinth: A square unmoulded block placed on the floor to receive the mouldings of an architrave.

Pulvinated frieze: A cushion-shaped or semicircular frieze.

Pylon: A monumental wall space usually terminating an arcade or colonnade.

Quarry: A light of glass in leaded glazing.

Quoins: Squared stones at the corners of buildings or of architectural features.

Racking: The face of masonry which is alternately indented in the coursing to receive a future masonry wall.

Rail: Horizontal members of panel frames. Guard on the outer edge of a stair or gallery.

Rake: Slope or pitch of a roof.

Rustication: Horizontal and vertical channels cut in the joints of stonework.

Scantling: Material used in framing; the dimensions of a piece of timber in breadth and thickness.

Scored: Surface of masonry which is scratched to make a bond for plaster.

Soffit: The lower horizontal face of any projecting feature.

Spandrel: The triangular space between the shoulder of an arch and the rectangular figure formed by a moulding; also the space between the shoulders of two adjoining arches.

Staff bead: The moulding on the outside of a window frame to hold the sash in position.

Stile: The vertical member of a panel frame.

Stretcher: The long face of a brick when laid horizontally.

String course: See Belt Course.

Surround: The stone or brick facing around a fireplace opening.

Swirl: A curve or twist at the termination of a rail or balustrade.

Terminal swirl: See Swirl.

Tooling: The surface obtained by working the face of stone with a tool.

Torus: A convex moulding, nearly semicircular in cross-section.

Tympanum: The triangular recessed space enclosed by the cornice which bounds a pediment.

Verge board: The board following the rake or slope of a gable underneath the overhanging shingle or slate.

Voussoir: One of the wedge-like stones which form an arch; the middle one is called a keystone.

Wash: Sloping portion of a chimney cap employed to carry the outer projection of the cap back to the line of the shaft. A sloping surface to shed rain from projections.

Water-table: A projection of the lower masonry or brickwork on the outside of a wall, usually at the first-floor line.

Weathering: The sloping portion of a chimney stack which carries the larger dimension of the base to the smaller dimension above. This surface is usually covered with brick laid horizontally flatwise, though in instances it is covered with clay, tile or stone.

BRAY MONUMENT, WILLIAMSBURG

Index

Abingdon Church, 31
Allen, Arthur, 21
Ambler, Jaquelin, 99, 119
Ambler, Mary, 100
Ampthill, xv, 37 et seq., 119, 120, 169, 173, 179
Arches, flat brick, 60, 100, 121, 142; flat brick with segmental soffit, 89; flat stone, 111; segmental brick, 21, 41, 60, 76
Architrave, brick, 90; gauged brick, 89
Armistead of Hesse, 99
Arnold, Benedict, 72, 87

Bacon, Nathaniel, 11, 21
Bacon's Castle, xv, 4, 5, 19 et seq., 32, 179
Bacon's Rebellion, 141
"Belinda" (Rebecca Burwell), 99
Belt course, see String courses
Belvedere, 71
Berkeley, 99, 111
Berkeley, Gov., 119
Berkeley, Lady, 11
Berkeley, Norborne (Lord Botetourt), 11
Berkeley, Sir William, 11, 13
Beverley, Robert, 141, 143
Beverley, Col. William, 141, 142
Bewdley, Lancaster County, 12
Blair, Rev. Mr., 51
Blair House, Archibald, Williamsburg, 48
Bland, Elizabeth, 141
Blandfield, 88, 91, 130, 139 et seq., 168, 173, 174, 183
Blue Ridge Mountains, 141
Bolection moulding, 90
Brafferton Hall, Williamsburg, xv, 40, 51, 53
Brandon, Prince George County, 91, 130
Braxton, Carter, 99
Bray Monument, Williamsburg, 188
Bremo, 119
Brick, rubbed, xv, 75, 90, 102, 142
Brick sizes, 60, 177
Brickwork, 13, 22, 32, 53, 88, 176; copings, 22; English bond, xv, 4, 12, 21, 32, 40, 41, 43, 75, 91, 100, 112, 121; Flemish bond, xv, 4, 12, 32, 33, 40, 41, 43, 53, 60, 75, 76, 88, 89, 100, 102, 112, 121, 142; gauged, 61, 76, 90; glazed headers, 4, 5, 40, 41, 60, 65, 76, 88, 102; ground dressings, 41; moulded, 33, 61; rubbed dressings, xv, 41, 43, 60, 88, 89, 101, 120, 142; window trim, 21
Bruton Parish Church, 40
Burlington, Lord, 65
Burwell family, 31
Burwell, Abigail, 40
Burwell, Carter, 99, 111
Burwell, Lewis, 31, 40
Burwell, Major Lewis, 31
Burwell, Nathaniel, 31, 99
Burwell, Rebecca, 99
Byrd, Anne, 71, 99, 111
Byrd, Evelyn, 71, 72
Byrd, Jane, 71
Byrd, Maria, 71
Byrd, Ursula, 141
Byrd, Wilhelmina, 71
Byrd, William I, 71, 141
Byrd, William II, 71, 72, 99
Byrd, William III, 71, 72, 77

Capitol, Williamsburg, xiii, xv, xvi, 39, 40, 88
Carter family, 99
Carter, Anne, 99, 111
Carter, Charles, 71, 99, 111, 112
Carter, Elizabeth, 31, 99
Carter, John, 99, 111
Carter, Judith, 99, 111
Carter, Landon, 71, 99, 111
Carter, Lucy, 99
Carter, Mary, 99
Carter, Robert ("King"), 99, 111
Carter, St. Leger Landon, 112
Carter's Creek, 31
Carter's Creek Plantation House (Fairfield), 31
Carter's Grove, xiv, xvi, 4, 31, 61, 65, 90, 91, 97 et seq., 111, 112, 113, 119, 166, 172, 173, 175, 181
Cary, Archibald, 39, 40, 119
Cary, Henry, 39, 53
Cary, Henry II, 40
Casement windows, 3, 5, 12, 22
Chamberlayne, Thomas, 71
Chapel, College of William and Mary, 40, 51
Charles, ship, 3
Chatsworth, 119
Chesapeake Bay, xiv
Chesterfield County, 39
Chickahominy River, 11
Chimneys, 3, 4, 5, 11, 41, 43, 60, 61, 65, 75, 76, 77, 90, 100, 101, 102, 120, 130, 141, 142, 152; double-stack, 32; six-stack, 22; stone, 152; T-shaped, 53; triple-stack, 21, 33, 35
Chimney caps, stone, 111
Chiswick Villa, 65
Christ Church, Lancaster County, 90
Cleve, xiv, 99, 109 et seq., 165, 173, 174, 182
College of William and Mary, xvi, 119; Main Building, xiii, xv, 4, 5, 12, 39, 51, 88, 90
Cornices, xv, 32, 35, 41, 43, 53, 65, 75, 88, 90, 101, 111, 120, 130, 152
Cornwallis, Lord, 119
Court House, Williamsburg, xv
Cromwell House, England, 39
Cupolas, 90
Curles, 119
Curles Neck, 21
Custis, Daniel Parke, 72
Custis, Col. John, 71

Dale, Sir Thomas, 119
Dandridge, Martha, 72
Dawson, Rev. William, 51
de la Warre, Lord, 71
Dogue Post Office, 111
Doors, 31, 61, 91, 130
Doorways, gauged brick, 88, 89, 90, 100, 101; stone, 72, 75, 112, 129, 152; wood, 120, 121
Dormers, 3, 5, 12, 35, 53, 75, 88, 100, 102
Dungeness, 119
Dunmore, Lord, 87
Dutch Gap, 119

Elizabeth City County, 3

Fairfield, xv, 5, 12, 22, 29 et seq., 40, 42, 165, 179
Falling Creek iron works, 39
Finials, 22, 73
Fithian's diary, 59
Fitzhugh family, 99
Floor Plans, a Comparison of Outline, 179

Gables, xv, 3, 4, 21, 22, 41, 102, 112
Galt House, Williamsburg, xv
Gardens, 3, 31, 72, 77, 127
Gate posts, stone, xvi
Gates, wrought-iron, 72

Index

Gateways, 73, 77
Glossary of Architectural Terms, 185
Gloucester County, 87
Governor's Palace, Williamsburg, xiii, xv, 39, 87, 88, 91
Greenspring, 4, 5, 9 et seq., 59, 179
Grilles, basement window, 53
Gunston Hall, 39, 111

Hadley, Thomas, xvi, 51
Harrison, Benjamin, 99, 119
Henrico (Henricopolis), 119
Henry, Patrick, 87
Hesse, 99
Hill, Elizabeth, 99
Horsmanden, Mary, 71
Horsmanden, Col. Warham, 71
House of Burgesses, 21, 59, 119, 151

Ice house, Rosewell, 91
Ironwork, gates, 73

Jail, Greenspring, 12
James River, xiv, 11, 39, 99, 119, 120
Jamestown, xiii, 4, 11, 39
Jefferson, Thomas, 99, 119

Keys, stone, arch, 89
Kimball, Fiske, Introduction by, xi
"King" Carter of Corotoman, 31, 99
King James, 119
Kitchens, 12
Knight, Col. William Carter, 119
Knights of the Golden Horseshoe, 141

Label mould, 22
Lafayette, General, 119
Latrobe, Benjamin, 11, 12
Leaded glass, Greenspring, 12
Lee, Arthur, 59
Lee, Fitzhugh, 59
Lee, Francis Lightfoot, 59, 127, 151
Lee, Hannah Ludwell, 59
Lee, Major Henry, 59
Lee, Ludwell, 151
Lee, Phillip Ludwell, 59
Lee, Richard (of England), 59
Lee, Richard Henry, 59, 151
Lee, Robert E., 59
Lee, Col. Thomas, 59, 65, 151
Lee, Thomas Ludwell, 59
Lee, William, 59
Lee, William Ludwell, 11, 13
Lee House, Greenspring estate, 15
Lewis, Fielding, 112
Loggia, stone, 128
Louis XVI, 53
Ludwell family, 59
Ludwell, Col. Phillip, 11, 59
Lynn, England, 3
Lynnhaven Bay, 3

MacDonald-Millar, Rev. Donald, 22
Mann, Mary, 87

Mantels, marble, 72
Map of Virginia, *Frontispiece*
Marble steps, 53
Marshall, John, 100
Mason, George, 39
Meade, Bishop, 90
Menokin, xvi, 90, 91, 127, 130, 149 et seq., 163, 164, 166, 167, 174, 183
Middle Plantation, 39
Minitree, David, xvi, 99, 112
Mordaunt, Charles, Earl of Peterborough, 72
Mount Airy, xvi, 91, 125 et seq., 141, 142, 143, 163, 166, 167, 170, 173, 175, 182
Mount Pleasant, 65
Mount Vernon, 60

Nelson House, Yorktown, 101, 111
Newels, wrought-iron, 53
Nicholson, Francis, 39
Nomini Hall, 99, 111

Octagon, Washington, D. C., The, 127
Offley, Sarah, 3
Orangery, 127
Orrery, Earl of, 72

Page family, 87
Page, John, 71, 87, 99
Page, Mann, 87, 99
Page, Mann II, 87
Page, Matthew, 87
Panelling, 4, 40, 111, 120, 142
Paradise, Gloucester County, 59
Parapets, 22, 88, 90, 111
Parke, Daniel, 71
Parke, Frances, 71
Parke, Lucy, 71
Paulett, Sir John, 71
Paulett, Thomas, 71
Pediments, 22, 53, 61, 89, 90, 101, 120, 128
Pembroke, Nansemond County, 40, 42
Petersburg, 71
Pilasters, 76, 89, 90, 101, 120
Plan, H, 60
Plan, L, 11, 31
Plan, U, 11, 41
Plans, A Comparison of Outline, 179
Plastering, 21
Pohick Church doorway, xvii
Porches, 13
Portraits, at Blandfield, 141; at Carter's Grove, 72; at Cleve, 111; at Westover, 72
Potomac River, xiv, 99
Powder Horn, Williamsburg, 40
President's House, College of William and Mary, xv, 40, 49 et seq., 88, 120, 170, 172, 173, 175, 179
Prestwould, Mecklenburg County, xvi

Princess Anne County, 3
Profiles, Full-size Details of, 161
Province House, The Boston, 22, 33

Quoins, 111, 112, 128, 129, 151

Randolph family, 39, 119
Randolph, Anne, 119
Randolph, Innes, 119
Randolph, John, 119
Randolph, Mary, 39, 119
Randolph, Peyton, 119
Randolph, William I, 119
Randolph, William III, 119
Rappahannock River, xiv, 99, 111, 141
Richmond, 71, 119
Roanoke, 119
Roofs, clipped gable, 60; deck on hip, 88, 90; flat, 90; hip, xv, 32, 43, 60, 65, 112, 120; hip on hip, 129, 141, 152; shingle, 53, 100; slate, 53, 75; triple hip, 42
Rookings, William, 21
Rosegill, Middlesex County, 99
Rosewell, xiv, xv, xvi, 31, 61, 85 et seq., 99, 111, 163, 165, 167, 170, 171, 173, 174, 181
Rustication, 112, 128, 130, 151

Sabine Hall, Richmond County, 99, 111
Sash, sliding, xv
Secretary's Office, Williamsburg, 35
Shingles, round-end, 42
Shirley, Charles City County, 88, 91, 99, 111, 130
Slavery, 11
Spotswood, Alexander, 141
St. Luke's Church, Isle of Wight County, xv, 4, 22
Stafford County Court House, xvi
Stair rails, wrought-iron, 53
Stairs, 111
Stairway, Chippendale, 152
Stark, Mrs., 59
Stegge, Capt. Thomas, 71
Steps, Georgian, 48; stone, xvi, 60, 75, 90, 100, 112, 128, 143
Stone, Aquia Creek, xvi, 53, 128; Portland, xvi, 53, 128; use of, xvi, 48, 73, 111, 112, 127, 128, 129, 151
Stratford, xiv, xv, 41, 57 et seq., 87, 88, 175, 180
String courses, 21, 32, 40, 41, 53, 88, 89, 100, 121, 129, 142
Stuart, Charles Edward, 59
Stuart, Dr. Richard, 59
Sweet Hall, King William County, 4

Tappahannock, town of, 141
Tarleton, Col., 100
Tayloe, Benjamin Ogle, 127
Tayloe, Col. John, 127, 151
Tayloe, The Misses, 127

[190]

Index

Tayloe, Rebecca, 127, 151
Tayloe, William H., 127
Taylor, Maria, 71
Tebbs House, Dumfries, 111
Thornton, Dr. William, 127
Thoroughgood, Adam, 3
Thoroughgood House, Adam, xv, 1 *et seq.*, 21, 22, 33, 41, 76, 102, 179
Thoroughgood, Sir John, 3
Tombs, Burwell, 31; at Rosewell, 87, 91; at Westover, 71, 77
Towers, 21
Tuckahoe, Goochland County, 60, 119
Turkey Island, 119
Tyttenhanger, England, 89

Urns, carved stone, 128

Varina, Henrico County, 119

Warren House (Rolfe House), Surry County, 53
Warsaw, 151
Washington, Betty, 112
Washington, Gen. George, 39, 72, 119
Washington, Martha, 71
Water-tables, 21, 41, 60, 65, 88, 89, 100, 102, 111, 112, 121, 142, 151
Weatherings, 4
West, Capt. Francis, 71
Westover, xiii, xv, 41, 69 *et seq.*, 87, 88, 99, 111, 120, 164, 167, 173, 175, 181
Westover Manuscripts, 71
Williamsburg, xiii, xiv, xv, 12, 39, 40, 87, 99

Willing, Mary, 72
Wilton, 39, 40, 76, 117 *et seq.*, 174, 176, 182
Window trim, stone, xvi, 151
Windows, casement, 3, 5, 12, 22; sash, 3, 21, 53, 90; segmental head, 43, 75; tracery, 4
Windowsills, moulded wood, 120; stone, 89, 111, 112
Wood houses, xv
Woodwork, 87, 100, 102, 111, 130, 142, 152
Wormeley, of Rosegill, 99
Wren, Sir Christopher, 51

York River, xiv, 31, 87
Yorktown, xiii, 101